OUR MISS WADLAND

By Shane Wadland

EDWARD GASKELL *publishers*
DEVON

Edward Gaskell *publishers*
6 Grenville Street
Bideford
Devon EX39 2EA

First Published 1999

ISBN: 1-898546-32-0

OUR MISS WADLAND

Printed & Bound by
Lazarus Press
Unit 7 Caddsdown Business Park
Bideford
Devon EX39 3DX

To my Mother

& the worthy people of Dolton

AMW

Alice Wadland pictured with some of her pupils, bathing in the River Torridge, by the Halsdon estate which was then the property of the Furse family. The photo was taken c.1925.
Of all the photos of Alice I have in my possession this is undoubtedly my favourite. It captures Alice in one of her few moments of relaxations.

AMW

CONTENTS

List of Illustrations
(between pages 96-97)

Miss Sarah Wadland, 'the favourite aunt'
Miss Alice Wadland, c.1930
The Wadland family
Mrs Eliza Wadland
Miss Sarah Wadland
Travelling bears in France c.1905
Margaret Wadland
Richard Wadland
Summer tea-party at Aller Court c.1907
Aller Church
Miss Kathleen Wadland
Alice's pet owl
Aller Court House
Henry Lawrence Wadland
Lt. R. A. Faire and Lt. E. G. Holyoak
Earliest known group photograph of Alice's pupils
Alice in the garden at Sages
Group photograph taken at Sages c.1954
The Matterhorn, Switzerland
Mountain range in the region of Lauterbrunnen
Alice Wadland
Mrs Eliza Wadland
Alice, her mother and sister Winifred
Elise Wadland
Kathleen Wadland c.1905
Alice Wadland
Sages, Dolton c.1920
Alice Wadland in Dolton village square
Alice's Letter to Evangeline Lynch-Blosse
Alice in the garden at Southover
Commemorative jug commissioned by the author

FOREWORD

I like many others had the privilege of sending my children to school with Alice Wadland in the nineteen sixties, and I shall always remember her kindness and particularly the lovely atmosphere that existed in her cottage in those days.

Shane Wadland's very interesting account of an age sadly left behind is an illustration of the strength of character of a Lady who throughout her life upheld true Christian principles.

It is also an important record of Parish life and activities which have taken place before and between two world wars, reflecting the lives of many people.

The trouble taken in the research and the many interesting anecdotes make it so well worth reading. I hope like me, you will find it most stimulating.

Lord Clinton

Heanton Satchville
Devonshire
1999

AMW

INTRODUCTION

This book is long overdue, and I apologise to those who have patiently waited for its release. However, the research undertaken required the utmost care, as I was deprived of certain lines of documentation. Principally, this biography is a tribute to a lady who established her own private school in rural North Devon. The lady in question was very much an individualist, with an inexhaustibly strong will, who never accepted defeatism, even with her own pupils, always the optimist, adamantly believing that anything was possible. She proved her point time and time again, in bringing out the hidden abilities of her pupils, identifying them as unique individuals who could go, and have gone on to lead successful lives. The person in question was Alice Mary Wadland.

Many of her former pupils and local residents only knew her as "Miss Wadland", and whilst compiling this book it was amusing to see the expression on some peoples' faces when told what her her Christian name was: To them, it seemed almost inconceivable that she had had any Christian names at all. In this book I tend to refer to her simply as Alice. The exception is where I quote various anecdotes and stories from her pupils, and other acquaintances. Being an individualist, Alice never (even as a child) liked being the centre of attention, usually retiring, and in her latter years disliked even the slightest publicity about her school, or her own interesting personal life.

This book is not going to be over factual, in the sense of stating endless statistics which tend to bore the average reader to tears. I think Alice's achievements are expressed in the thoughts of her pupils, through their edifying memoirs. I also hope that in the following pages I have expressed the uniqueness of her school, and the calibre of person that she was. Alice's teaching career spanned 51 years, in the village of Dolton which went through two World Wars, saw four different British monarchs, great educational changes in 1944, many domestic changes of post-war Britain (2nd World War), and then onto and through the 'wayward' 1960s.

I decided to devote most of my time to Alice, as she is one of the more interesting members of the Wadland family. Many people with whom I have come into contact with, speak of Alice with great admiration and respect. Undoubtedly, she has left a great impression on many peoples' lives, even 26 years after her death, and this I think is a most commendable accolade.

My curiosity in Alice started back in the summer of 1983, when, with my parents, I came up from our family home in Cornwall and headed for the parish of Merton as my father wanted to visit an area of land on Lord Clinton's estate where there was activity of red deer, and where my father intended to do some shooting. After our visit there we were planning to head back to Cornwall, when en-route my father pointed out the turning for Dolton (off the A386 road) and said that this was the place where our forebears came from. So, we turned off and went through the scenic countryside and then crossed New Bridge (over the river Torridge), through the hamlet of Langham, and finally arriving in Dolton village. We spoke to one or two locals who knew our relatives, the deceased Misses Wadland. We went into Dolton churchyard and found various ancestral gravestones,and the more recent one of Alice and her sister Kathleen Wadland. From that initial visit, I fell for Dolton and savoured its atmosphere.

There were subsequent visits, some with friends, and the first person I was introduced to (who knew the Misses Wadland well) was Miss Beattie Friend, who in turn introduced me to the late Jack Mardon, a marvellous character with great local knowledge and flowing with endless tales. I visited Jack Mardon on several further occasions, and he told me some fascinating stories about Alice, and before long I realised what an interesting individual she was. I delved more and more into her life, and then finally took the decision to write her biography. It was a pity that I never met Alice. I was aged 7 when she died. Even if I had known her, I doubt whether I would have appreciated the sort of person she was.

On one particular visit to Dolton (1984) with my sister Sally, we were in the village having a good look around, and enquiring about anyone who might have known Alice or Kathleen. Sally and I parted company, and after about half an hour, we met up back in the village square. My sister reappeared from one of the business premises, and was in the middle of having a good laugh. She said that she had been talking to one particular individual who knew Alice and Kathleen in their latter years, and the response from the person was, "Oh them, the Wadlands! they were just a pair of snobs!" I was rather indignant at that remark, but my sister thought it thoroughly amusing. The individual who made that remark has never been known for her diplomacy. The person obviously did not know Alice and Kathleen in any great depth. Admittedly I did relent and saw the amusing side of the situation, and ended it by brushing the comment aside, and just concluded that we are *all* snobs at heart, something which the English are renowned for.

On reflection Alice and Kathleen may have been a little snobbish, but it's not that surprising when you consider their middle-class background. As children they were privileged enough to have had servants, and several estate workers. In her early womanhood Alice made it quite clear to her household staff what their duties were, and to keep to their own place. In her view familiarity did breed contempt. Thankfully, as the years passed Alice mellowed, but at the same time she 'never suffered fools gladly'. Underneath the hard outer shell, Alice was a most considerate, charitable, fair and warm human being, and also had a wonderful sense of humour. It was never in her character to intentionally hurt anyone. Alice and Kathleen knew how to conduct themselves, and were simply two decent and unpretentious ladies.

Writing Alice's biography has indeed been a challenge.

For a biographer fortunate enough to meet his subject face to face it is an ideal opportunity of getting to know the thoughts, moods and inner spirit of the individual. However, through perseverance, I can say with confidence that I have reached Alice's inner spirit. Sadly many of the family letters were destroyed which leaves a dent in building an even stronger picture of the family structure. Also, as far as I know, no diaries exist but I think it very unlikely that Alice would ever have had time to keep one. Alice was also a good amateur artist, having an excellent sense of perspective but sadly, as far as I know nothing survives of her artistic talents.

I thought that the title of the book most appropriate because as Alice lived for most of her life in Dolton, several people in the village used to, and still do, refer to her affectionately as 'Our Miss Wadland'.

Oscar Wilde once said, "Every great man nowadays has his disciples, and it is always Judas who writes the biography." I certainly hope that Alice would not have seen me in the same light. I would like to think that she would have been rather touched that someone had put pen to paper, not so much for her own personal vanity, but having made a record of a little known private school, for the sake of posterity.

I am very much indebted to Mr Jack Mardon, his wife Mabel (who as a girl was taught the piano by Alice), their son Derek, and Derek's son and daughter-in-law Keith and Tracey, who have all been extremely helpful during my searches, providing an abundant source of information on Alice. I only regret that Jack Mardon is no longer with us to see this book. If it had not been for Jack and Mabel's foresight in retrieving much of the school records, most of them would almost certainly have been lost forever.

An ardent thanks goes to the people of Dolton for their enthusiasm, contribution and support, and this also includes Mrs Maud Fishleigh, who from time to time chased me up on the progress of the book. A sincere thanks goes to my cousins Nancy Leverton and Kathleen Hawkey for their much appreciated support.

A most grateful thanks goes to the following individuals and societies: Margery Rowe, John Draisy, Tim

14

Wormleighton, and all their colleagues at the Devon Record & North Devon Record Offices; the librarians of the West Country Studies Library in Exeter, the churchwardens of Roborough Church, the head and staff at Badminton school in Bristol, and another indebted thanks goes to all of Alice's former pupils who responded to my questionnaire with such enthusiasm and helped considerably in establishing a rich tapestry of what happened during daily life at the school and of the person who was its *magnum opus*.

Finally a loving thanks goes to my mother and Gill Stevens, who patiently helped to edit this book.

Shane Wadland
Dolton
1999

A M W

MISS ALICE MARY WADLAND
(1892 - 1972)

Alice was born on the 16th of September 1892 (one of 7 children), in the parish of Roborough at the family estate of Owlacombe*, the daughter of Richard and Eliza Wadland, a middle-class yeoman family with an ancient Devonian lineage. Alice was baptised 15th October 1892 at the Anglican Church of St Peter, Roborough, by the Reverend Reginald Mortimer who was a personal friend of the Wadlands. Alice's great-grandfather Samuel Wadland, 'gentleman', acquired Owlacombe in the early part of the 19th century from the Rolle family of Stevenstone. The property passed indirectly down to Alice's father Richard. He eventually sold the estate in 1900.

Richard with his young family moved to one of their other properties called Down Farm (which had been vacated by tenants), in the parish of Beaford for about a year. After their short occupation of Down, the family prepared for their move to the parish of Aller, in the county of Somerset (information about their time in Somerset is farther on in this book).

The Wadlands' time at Owlacombe was a happy one, particularly for the children as they had so much freedom with all the space around them, and the family often entertained. Owlacombe was very much a hive of activity.

*Owlacombe was the Wadlands' home farm and as well as owning other property within the parish of Roborough, they possessed other tenanted farms, properties and lands in the parishes of Beaford, Shebbear and Winkleigh. On the death of Richard Wadland's father Henry in 1871, the entire estate was divided between Richard and his two elder brothers Samuel and Henry, and that is when Richard came into possession of Owlacombe. Owlacombe was anciently known as 'Over Woolacombe'. For centuries after the Norman Conquest it was the home of the illustrious Woolacombe family.

However all was not rosy, particularly in the line of agriculture which in the latter part of the 19th century was going through a depression. Richard and Eliza also realised that with the arrival of the 20th century there were many cultural and educational changes, and they accepted the fact that North Devon was rather isolated, especially when it came to considering the future of their children and deciding what schools to send them to. The choice of private schools in North Devon was rather restricted, particularly for girls, so this was the main reason for their eventual move to Somerset as it was within easy distance of the Great Western Railway leading to Bristol and beyond.

Alice and her siblings whilst at Owlacombe, and then Aller Court, had their own private governess as it was regarded not befitting for the children to attend the local primary schools (ie Roborough and Aller) which would have meant mixing with the local children, several of whom had fathers or relatives who worked on the estates for the Wadland family. It was very much a 'them and us' attitude. When the Wadland children finished their preparatory education, they were sent onto the appropriate private schools. The children didn't lead a solitary life, far from it, they had several cousins who they would meet up with on a fairly regular basis, as well as making friends with children whose parents socialised with Richard and Eliza. Usually once a year (during the summer), the Wadlands would lay on a tea party for the estate workers and tenants and their immediate families which involved a multitude of people. Fun was had by all, particularly the children. Party games were organised and the Wadland children would participate but usually they were on the sidelines, being the organisers, ever mindful of how to conduct themselves.

AN IDEAL SETTING

The parish of Dolton is situated on the fringe of North Devon; hilly country with scattered farms, picturesque wooded valleys and meandering streams. On high ground, Dolton parish lies between Dartmoor and Exmoor, catching some bracing winds as well as its fair share of rain. The land is good and fertile with a rich variety of flora and fauna, with occasional sightings of hares darting about, and frequent sightings of red and roe deer, mainly in and around the woodlands.

The famous river Torridge runs alongside the west of the parish with its tranquil waters flowing past wooded banks, grazing sheep in meadows and an abundance of bird life with the occasional glimpse of the darting kingfisher. The river was once well known for its otters. Sadly with over hunting (which used to have meets in Dolton village) they soon diminished in numbers. However, today thankfully, there is a gradual increase in the population.

The old part of Dolton village has a charm and character of its own, with its tiny streets, thatched cobbed cottages and typical English gardens with the occasional apple tree. Dolton is where Alice Wadland lived for 55 years of her life, and as mentioned previously, spent 51 of those years running her own school. Dolton was once a rather isolated community with most of the old local families (known as Doltonians) being related to one another. The majority of the workforce were connected with agriculture, either employed on the two local estates of Halsdon & Stafford, or else working for the yeoman.

Although isolated, Dolton was very self-supporting with a multitude of small businesses in the village which included its own bank, resident doctor, cobbler, blacksmith, ironmonger and baker. The 1st and 2nd World Wars changed all of that, and after the last war Dolton saw an influx of people from other parts of Britain with an ever decreasing number of true Doltonians (born and bred), until the community has virtually become cosmopolitan. Now the majority of people travel into the towns and cities to work but they enjoy returning to Dolton which is well known for its friendly and lively community, yet at the same time it's a place where one can find peace.

IN THE BLOOD

In 1898 the death occurred of Miss Ann Wadland, on the 5th of January. Ann Wadland was a 2nd cousin to Alice's father and she had appointed him executor of her estate. Ann was born in Dolton in 1836 (the daughter of Henry Wadland 1786-1856) and for all her life she lived in the parish. She was a very charitable woman, and she also took a particular interest in local education, and was very supportive of the 'Village Voluntary School' (now known as the P C Primary School), with a deep concern that all children had the right of access to education. Over her lifetime Ann built up an impressive library of books, and in her Will she bequeathed her whole library to the school, with the added entailment that the people of Dolton also had access to the collection. She also bequeathed her resident property to the school. Ann's Will, in part, through its trust is still active to this day (nearly 100 years later) as the primary school receives a small amount of money each year, although with present day inflation the amount does not have much impact now. A complete extract of Ann's will can be found on page 149

Ann's immediate family consisted of one brother and two sisters, all of whom had died many years previously and at no great age. So as her next closest living kinsman was Richard Wadland, she took particular interest in Richard's children and saw the brightness and potential in Alice and her sisters.

Another Miss Wadland who had an involvement in education was Alice's aunt Sarah Wadland, a very refined lady and of immense integrity. Sarah, like Alice was born at Owlacombe, Roborough, and for most of her life she lived in the parish of Beaford. Sarah was for many years a governor of the 'Beaford School Board' and took much interest in the welfare of the local children. So the line of Wadland women connected with education was there in the blood, and was to continue in strength with Alice and some of her sisters.

Alice was particularly fond of Sarah, both of similar natures, and often at weekends Alice would go and stay with her, usually cycling over to Beaford. Alice never learnt to drive a car but if she wanted to get around the immediate vicinity she would then use her bicycle. Occasionally she would be seen heading for Roborough village (approximately 5 miles away), when she was collecting the rent or inspecting her cottages. On one occasion Alice was heading back from Roborough, in heavy rain, when Alan Parsley (a respected local builder) was heading back to Dolton in his builders van. On seeing Alice absolutely drenched he stopped to ask whether she wanted a lift. This offer immediately put her on guard, with an expression as if to say, "a man offering me a lift?" Suspiciously, she looked at the person who made the offer, and when totally satisfied with who it was, accepted with much gratitude. Alan Parsley said with amusement that had he been a total stranger, "Miss Wadland would probably have given me one of her blackest looks and cycled on, no matter what the weather."

AN OLD BADMINTONIAN

The Wadlands' move to the parish of Aller in Somerset, occurred in 1902. Aller is situated in the heart of the county, approximately two and a half miles north-west of the town of Langport. Alice's parents lived at Aller Court, and farmed an active agricultural estate comprising approximately 400 acres of lowland, as well as farming some land in the neighbouring parish of Ham. Alice's time spent at Aller Court was rather short, usually at weekends, and school holidays.

As previously mentioned, one of the main reasons for the move to Somerset was that it was within easy commuting distance of Bristol, which was the place where Alice, and three of her sisters were to be educated. The girls were weekly boarders at Badminton House School in Clifton. After their breaks at home, the girls would be taken to the railway station at Langport West, where they caught the train which would take about an hour to get into Westbury-on-Trym (one of the main railway junctions) and then catch arranged transport which took them on to Badminton School.

The parish of Aller has a mixture of plains and wooded hills, and an endless sight of orchards; a most wonderful prospect when blossoming in the spring. Close to the village, with its old red bricked buildings and weeping willow trees, one can hear in the nearby woods the beautiful chorus of nightingales. This must have been a delight to Alice and her sisters; a time for young Edwardian ladies during their school breaks to explore this pleasant land. The Wadland girls were keen on cycling, and would often go off riding with friends who were staying with them from school.

Badminton House School at that time was situated at Worcester Terrace*. Badminton School was founded in 1858, by a Mrs Badcock. It was established as a small private school for girls in Burlington Gardens, Clifton. Alice's headmistress was a Miss Bartlett (a former pupil at Badminton), who was there from c.1895 to 1911. In 1911, the school saw the arrival of new head called Beatrice May Baker (born 4th May 1876, in the county of Hereford), who became very much part of the fabric of Badminton School. Obviously, by the time miss Baker got to Badminton, Alice had already left, but her two younger sisters, Margaret and Elsie were under Miss Baker's authority.

Badminton boasted several notable pupils, many from very different walks of life, although the majority were from middle class families. One very distinguished Badmintonian was Indira Nehru, (later becoming Mrs Gandhi, Prime Minister of India), who after leaving Badminton corresponded with Miss Baker on a regular basis which gave Miss Baker much pleasure. Miss Baker was rather casual in her dress, yet, she was apparently a strict disciplinarian, and on entering a classroom "total silence immediately ensues." Very much the same effect which Alice had on her pupils!

In the summer of 1914, Elsie (the youngest daughter of Richard and Eliza Wadland) completed her education at Badminton, aged 16. By this time Winifred, Kathleen and Alice were well into their teaching careers. Richard and Eliza were justifiably proud of their achievement in giving their daughters the opportunity of acquiring a first class education, and the fruits of their labours were further crowned when Alice demonstrated what capabilities she had to offer the educational world.

§

*In 1924, Badminton House School left Clifton, moving to the neighbouring district of Westbury-on-Trym, where the school has been running ever since, and has an international reputation.

> *Good, better, best*
> *Never be at rest*
> *'Till our good is better*
> *and our better best.*

Alice adopted this piece of verse during her teens, which perhaps would appear rather precocious for a youngster. Nevertheless, it certainly reflected her capable and attainable aspirations.

This engaging little ink drawing was characteristic of what Kathleen and her sisters would draw for one another during their Edwardian childhood.

THE GOVERNESSES

In 1915, Alice went into the employment of Bertram Frederick Trelawney Hare Esq, as a private governess to his daughter Clarice "Violet" Hare at the family home of Curtisknowle, in Diptford, South Devon. Alice remained at Curtisknowle until 1917. The Curtisknowle estate comprised of 1,774 acres, and was an active agricultural estate with several tenanted farms. The Hares of Curtisknowle were a minor branch of a larger family, who originated from the county of Cork in Ireland. They left Ireland c.1720, and settled in Bristol, where they became prosperous merchants. William Hare (1757-1820) bought Curtisknowle in the late 18th century. The estate was in the family until 1946, when it was then sold. The manor house is situated in a delightful setting, typically English, looking out towards the Avon valley, with superb views of other valleys steeped in woodland. At the bottom of the main valley flows the river Avon, or as it is known locally, the "Aun".

As a governess Alice was paid £25 per annum, which was regarded at that time quite a princely sum. Violet Hare was a most charming and agreeable girl, with fine flowing ginger hair and striking blue eyes. She was born on the 23rd October 1908 at the family home, and was then baptised on the 9th December in the same year. She was the youngest of three, having two brothers. By the time Alice became governess Violet was nearly aged eight years old.

On the 10th March 1917, Alice left the service of the Hare family, returning to North Devon, and moved in with her recently widowed mother in Dolton. This then allowed Alice time for preparations for the opening of her school in the autumn. Alice and Violet kept in contact with each other for the rest of their lives.

From 1900 onwards, Alice's elder sisters were also beginning to establish themselves in the teaching profession; May Wadland was the first of the girls to go into teaching, however, I shall come back to her later. Winifred became a gym mistress and spent the greater part of her working life in Leicestershire and Lancashire. When Kathleen completed her education at Badminton in 1906, she went straight into teaching English and French, proving to have very competent teaching abilities. During her early career Kathleen went into the employment of the higher echelons, ie as private governess to the daughters of aristocratic and landed gentry families, within the county of Devon. From 1919 to 1920, Kathleen lived in Honiton where she became governess to the Ladies Evelyn, Mary and Kathleen Courtenay, daughters of Frederick Leslie Courtenay who at that time was the Rector of Honiton and later became the 16th Earl of Devon.

Lady Mary Courtenay gave me this brief account of Kathleen; "I remember Miss Wadland quite well, she was very kind but strict, and it was a very happy time that she was with us." By Lady Mary's remarks, Kathleen was obviously very much like Alice in temperament, but was even more reserved. After Kathleen's departure from the Courtenay's she went to teach in various girls' public schools in England, sticking to her particular forte of English and French. In her latter years of retirement Kathleen returned to Devon and spent the remainder of her life living with Alice.

For a short period Margaret Wadland also went into teaching, and in 1912 she returned to her native parish of Roborough, and became governess to Richard Birdwood and his sister who were living at Ebberley House which belonged to the Birdwoods' grandparents Mr and Mrs Davis. Margaret remained in the employment of the family until 1914. Her role was principally to be nursery governess to the Birdwood children, as their mother had died when they were young (although Richard Birdwood was aged seven when Margaret became his mentor in 1912), and their father Lt-Col Gordon Birdwood was at the time serving in British India. I had the pleasure of meeting

Lt-Col Richard Birdwood at his home in 1992; a most charming and considerate gentleman. His memories of Margaret had rather faded, but he did say that he was "very fond of her".

Of all the Wadland girls, Margaret was the sweetest and gentlest, very much of her mother's disposition, however, this was not particularly to her own advantage as she was one that could not deal with crowds easily, and maybe this was the reason why she gave up teaching. She happily spent the rest of her working life in a very good secretarial job in London. I understand from a relative that she worked for the architect Sir Giles Gilbert Scott (1880-1960).

SACRIFICED AND ONLY 33

Many of Alice's attitudes and actions were typically Victorian, born during a decade when the British Empire was at its height, educated during the closing stages of the Victorian era, and overlapping into the Edwardian years. With the outbreak of the hideous First World War (1914-1918) this was a turbulent time within the Wadland family. It has never been proven with absolute clarity, but local tradition had it that as well as Alice tragically losing her brother (known to the family as Harry) she had a boyfriend who also died in the war. The family lost several other acquaintances, some of Alice's sisters had "gentlemen friends" who they also grievously lost, including one young officer who was gassed. Alice was very fond of her brother Henry, although there was eight years difference between them. Henry was a most charming and peaceful individual, taking more after his mother's character, and he absolutely doted on all his young sisters.

On the outbreak of the war, Henry decided to join up, however he failed his medical, thus denying him a place in the British Army. I believe the reason for this was that his eyesight was poor, and had to wear glasses for reading. This did not perturb him, and he made it quite clear to his family that he would find some opening. So, he left England, and sailed for Canada where he did manage to enter the army. He entered the Russel B Detachment as a private, training to become a member of the mounted yeomanry. His regiment was eventually sent to Europe, right into the horrors of the western front.

Obviously whilst on the continent, he corresponded with various members of his family, and in September 1917 he wrote to his sister Winifred. It is believed that this was the last time he wrote to a member of his family before he was seriously wounded in action on 6th November at Passchendaele, and four days later died of his injuries. The letter that he had sent to Winifred was found after Alice's death, amongst her treasured possessions and a transcript of it reads as follows:

22nd Sept 1917

My Dear Winnie,

Many thanks for your letter which I received a week or two ago. Have been away about a month, your letter was forwarded on. Would like a pair or two of socks if you wish to send them. Please send them if you can by return post, if it will not inconvenience you. Have just written to mother. Pte.H.L.Wadland 1000440 16th Canadian Scottish Batt, attached to 1st Canadian Infantry Batt France.

We have been having good weather the last week or two, guess you are back in Leicester now till Xmas holidays. Well I do not think I have much more news so will close with love to you and Elsie. From your loving brother.

Henry

Obviously Henry's death at only thirty-three was of great devastation to his mother and sister, and none of them ever really recovered from the loss of their "dearest Harry". Years after his death, Alice would now and again reflect on her brother, and her eyes seemed to express the futility and pain of those torn years, and the fact that she had lost something irreplaceable. However, the family kept their sanity and that was due to their faith. Alice had a very deep sense of the spiritual; and was the main strength for her mother.

Alice's mother was the recipient of the following letter. Nothing is known about the nephew who wrote it, not even his surname, as he was connected on Eliza's side of the family, ie the Voddens. One can only hope that his fate was kinder than his poor cousin's.

Sunday 3rd December 1917
9.30 pm

My dear Aunt Eliza

    Yesterday evening brought me the worst tidings I have had for some considerable time.

    I received a letter from the survivor informing me that my cousin Harry had been killed in action. He could not give me any details and I am now wondering whether the tragedy occurred on my front or elsewhere. I believe somehow that it is in our particular sector as I came across many men of the same regiment as the one to which Harry belonged but perhaps it was not his Battalion. At the time I was not in possession of mother's letter containing Harry's address. I expect I shall be receiving more details in the next letter.

    It was only a few days ago I looked up Harry's address in my note book and intended writing to him with the object of locating him. However, I am afraid I will never have the pleasure of realising my wish.

    My dear Aunt I can quite conceive how grieved you all must be and I must admit I myself out here feel the pain very much indeed. You have only one consolation and that is of knowing he died as a hero, doing his duty nobly for King and Country. You have my most heartfelt sympathy and I share with you the grief in this sad bereavement.

    How are Aunt Mary and all? I hope all right!

    Pluck up courage and be brave, the only way to lessen the pain.

With best love and kisses.
Your affectionate nephew,
George.

Will write again soon!

The military sent back Henry's belongings, including his Canadian Bible, and identity disc. Henry's mother was next of kin, and she was sent the silver Canadian memorial cross. The family also received the General Service and Victory medals, as well as the British Memorial Plaque, with the motto "He Died for Honour and Freedom", all of which, I now have in my possession.

Also during the war years – on the 5th of January 1916 – Alice's sister "Miss May" died. May was also a teacher, an extremely intelligent and gifted woman, but sadly (the exact reasons of which are unknown to me), she was institutionalised at the County Asylum, Exminster, where she died. After her death, her body was driven by 'motor hearse'* back to North Devon, and interred at Roborough churchyard, in the Wadland family burial ground.

In addition to the above, Alice's father Richard Wadland also died the same year, on the 3rd of December, and not under particularly happy circumstances, due to Richard's final downfall through drink. Undeniably, Richard was an extremely clever and caring man, but in his latter years the drink started to take its hold, then things went from bad to worse, when at one stage during his alcoholism he even started gambling his lands away. His death though sorrowful must have been in other ways a merciful release, as it was humiliating for Eliza, the way in which he was becoming aggressive in public. Local elderly people can remember him when he would be seen coming out of the Royal Oak, rather the worse for wear. An imposing figure, he would start waving his cane stick at any cheeky children, and shouting that if he caught them, he would give them a good hiding. This just provoked the children into more antagonism. After Alice's death, a bottle of sealed 'Gordon's Gin' was found in a cupboard. It had belonged to her father, and was a sharp and grievous reminder of what it had done to him. After the whole distasteful experience with her father, Alice vowed never to touch drink, and became a teetotaller.

Referring back to Alice's post as governess at Curtisknowle, any unoccupied time that she had or was allowed (usually at the weekends), was spent travelling around south Devon, and sometimes meeting with friends and relatives. Another point of destination for Alice was visiting her sister May, in the County Asylum. Alice had known happier times with May, and she found it particularly heart-rending to see her sister in her deteriorating mental condition, but despite that, Alice continued visiting her sister on a regular basis, giving her elder sister tender

*The full burial details can be found on page 148

love and respectful consideration. She was painfully aware that May's ever downward spiralling health was leading to an obvious conclusion, and it made it all the harder for the rest of the family to accept the impending parting of one who was comparatively young, and that by an unforeseen act of nature was cruelly robbed of her sanity. Some of Alice's sisters found it very hard emotionally to handle the situation. Alice's brother Henry showed immense concern for May's condition, whilst their father Richard, though loving, found it hard to come to terms with the circumstances, and would simply refuse to talk about May in company, other than his immediate family.

With all her trials during the war years, Alice remained very much the optimist, and fought on with zest and hope, and I think I can safely say that by the end of 1918, she had well established her school, and had decided to commit her life purely to teaching, in service of others. It is quite an accomplishment to think that when she died at the age of 80, she had taught for about 60 years of her life. When Armistice was declared (the end of the 1st World War), there was great jubilation in Dolton, and when the news finally reached Alice, it was obviously of immense relief and joy to her and her mother though tinged with some bitterness. On hearing the news Alice headed off to Dolton Church for a thanksgiving service, the village was alive with activity, and the exaltation of the ringing of the Church bells.

WHY DOLTON?

One question which a number of people have put to me is why did Alice return to North Devon to take up teaching in Dolton? "Someone of her calibre could have progressed to be a headmistress of a large private school somewhere up country." Well, from talking to certain elderly ladies (who were Alice's earliest pupils), I got the impression that Alice wanted to give local girls the chance of having a good education, and opening their horizons and opportunities to the greater world.

Alice was truly a remarkable and gifted woman. She had an amazing ability of teaching virtually all manner of subjects, and also had a flare for languages and spoke French fluently. On average, she had about fifteen pupils at any one time in her class and she could switch without trouble from one child to the next giving guidance and instruction, even with the added consideration of the child's age and intellect. At times, Alice appeared ruthless in pushing some children beyond their abilities but she knew their limits. When Alice started her school, most of her pupils were daughters of local yeomen. Alice discernably saw potential in many of her pupils, and she would persevere in bringing out their talents. One such girl was Irene Lemon, who came from a yeoman family in the parish of Roborough.

Alice taught Irene the piano, and the child passed all her grades, then at the age of sixteen, Irene went to London and studied at the Royal Academy of Music. After finishing at the Academy, Irene taught the piano professionally. Another girl who was gifted musically was Edith Shute-Friend (a pupil from 1917-1923) and she also went on to teach the piano from her home in Dolton. Many of Alice's pupils now live throughout Britain and the world, several of whom lead very interesting and fulfiling careers. Those whom I managed to track down have often said that "Miss Wadland" left a great impression on their lives and greatly influenced their thoughts and actions.

By the 2nd World War, Alice had well and truly established her school, and by this time she had gained respect in a wider area and had an extensive cross section of pupils. It was now not just children from farming stock, but children from aristocratic, clergy, medical and military families. Then by the late 1940s, with Alice's reputation spreading, there was an influx of children from the nearby town of Great Torrington, coming mostly from business families.

Latin was not part of the weekly curriculum, however Alice did give individual instruction (after school hours) in the subject to any children who needed or requested some elementary grounding before they moved on to a public school. The rate Alice charged for extra tuition after school hours was a guinea (£1.05) a term, and this rate also applied to piano lessons.

A RIGHTFUL VOTE AT 33

In 1925, Alice finally had her first and rightful chance to vote. This is one thing that she passionately believed in having every right to do, although by the time she exercised her right she was aged 33. This right for women was thanks to the suffragettes, who made it possible with the birth of the Reform Voting Act which was passed in 1918.

Alice's views with regard to the Church and its functions were quite clear and principled. She was once known for giving a visiting clergyman to Dolton Church the cold shoulder for the fact that he had not worn his surplus whilst officiating the service. This was to Alice most improper, "a man of the cloth should know better than that!" Those who knew Alice well will vouch that just her look of disapproval or annoyance was enough to sort out an individual, and heaven help them if they ever stood out of line again.

A fundamentalist, Alice had very clear and strong convictions of her Christian faith. She was earnest in her teaching, an ardent reader of the Bible and absolute in preaching the Gospel. Alice took a very active part in church activities, being the organist in Dolton St Edmund's for forty-nine years, and later in life she took charge of the flower rota. In the 1920s she was a member of the Parochial Church Council. Then around 1926, she became the organiser of the local 'Girls' Friendly Society'. This society was linked to the Anglican Church and about six girls would meet up on a Saturday morning, and visit the elderly and sick in the parish to carry out any essential chores. The Dolton group disbanded in the late 1930s. Several of Alice's former pupils have often said that the church meant everything to her; "a most Godly woman", and in turn, her faith and rationality had rubbed off onto them.

The 'Girls' Friendly Society' was founded in 1875 and its object was 'To unite for the Glory of God in one Fellowship of Prayer & Service, the Girls & Women of the Empire to uphold Purity in thought, word and deed.' In its promotional campaign, the following was publicised:

> *"The Society offers friendly comradeship and opportunities of service for others, through introductions from branch to branch and from one country to another. It also encourages loyalty and faithfulness in work and home life, and self-control in all things."*

I thought that the last few words sounded rather ominous!

§

The following was written by Alice in one of her school registers. It typifies her thought and expression and was probably used as a grace.

> *Jesus grant us every day*
> *The nourishment we need,*
> *Earthly food and heavenly food,*
> *Body and soul to feed.*

KINDRED SPIRITS & MOUNTAINEERS

Of all her sisters Alice was particularly close to Kathleen, who would often come down to Devon during her summer holidays and stay with Alice. They would visit relatives, friends and did much sightseeing. The other sisters would also come down now and again. Winifred would occasionally appear on the scene. She was very much the extrovert of all the girls and always very gregarious and fashion conscious compared to Alice who was the opposite. Alice absolutely detested smoking, which was a vice of Winifred's. When she came for a holiday, Alice would not allow "Winnie" to smoke in her house. Winifred either had to go out into the garden, or into the village. She usually chose the latter, and she would often be seen walking around the village enjoying a cigarette.

Even Alice's living standards by the 1960s were, to many, quite humble and old fashioned. Alice was never extravagant or frivolous. If she bought anything, it had to be a necessity and not something on a whim. Her frugality seemed to be the result of the way in which her father was a total spendthrift. Richard spent most of his wealth, and upon his death left his family rather impoverished. Alice soon realised that she had to become the breadwinner, to support her mother, although Alice's sisters also rallied. Ultimately Richard paid for his mistakes by being disinherited by his wealthy uncle Samuel Wadland who died in 1910. However in his will, Samuel had not forgotten Richard's children.

One favourite destination for Alice and Kathleen during their holidays was Europe. From the early 1920s to the mid 1930s, they often travelled the continent, and Alice particularly loved Switzerland. She had visited most of the famous sites in the country, and with her sister Kathleen, did quite a lot of mountaineering. On the 3rd of August 1923, they arrived and spent time at a village called Lauterb.unnen* (2,640 ft), a pleasure resort in the Bernese Oberland and which is noted for its mountain torrents and breathtaking waterfalls. This region is outstanding for some of the most beautiful of Swiss scenery. While touring the Oberland (an area covering 1,800 square miles), they stayed at another resort called Murren which is three miles from Lauterbrunnen. Murren (5,000ft), is the highest village of the Bernese Oberland. Most impressive, it stands on cliffs 2,600 ft high above the Lauterbrunnen valley. Steeply rising peaks and glaciers in its immediate vicinity, make Murren a unique and unforgettable sight. The village is a good centre for the ascent of the Jungfrau (13,632ft). The Jungfrau is undoubtably the most beautiful of the Swiss mountains, as well as the most accessible, and was climbed by Alice and Kathleen. Their holiday over, it was time to head back home. They crossed Europe and arrived back in Dieppe, Belgium on the 24th of August, then crossed the channel for England, arriving home in time to start preparations for their new school terms.

On the 29th of August 1931, Alice and Kathleen visited Bologne after another holiday spent on the continent. Before their arrival in Bologne, they visited Estaple Military Cemetery (20 miles south of Bologne) to see their brother's grave and this was no doubt a rather emotional time for them.

On one of her earlier visits to Switzerland, Alice, with Kathleen travelled throughout the Canton of Valais. In the latter part of the journey they passed through the scenic valley of Val d'Annivers**, and then finally arriving at the resort of Zermatt which is a well known destination for mountaineers who intend to climb the famous triangular shaped and awe inspiring Matterhorn*** (14,688 ft). The Matterhorn is known to the French-Swiss as the Cervin. While staying in the resort, Alice and Kathleen joined a party of climbers, and both successfully climbed the Matterhorn. This was undoubtedly one of their most memorable achievements.

*Lauterbrunnen is eight miles from Interlaken, which is the gateway to the Bernese Oberland.

**The local people of this valley are of ancient Saracen descent.

***The Matterhorn was first climbed in 1865 by Edward Whymper.

THE MATTERHORN
TWILIGHT

"The time may come when the Matterhorn shall have passed away, and nothing save a heap of shapeless fragments will mark the spot where the great mountain stood; for atom by atom, inch by inch, and yard by yard, it yields to forces which nothing can withstand. That time is far distant and ages hence; generations unborn will gaze upon its awful precipices and wonder at its unique form. However exalted may be their ideas, and however exaggerated their expectations, none will come to return disappointed!"

Edward Whymper

THE BEGINNING –
ARSCOTTS (1917-1930)

When Alice started her school in 1917, she set aside a room in Arscotts*, for her pupils. There was plenty of room in the property, as it was now just Alice and her mother Eliza. Alice ran the school from Arscotts until1930, when she finally decided that the schoolroom was becoming too small with the growing number of pupils. Also, interest was spreading fast with more people asking Alice whether they could send their children to her school.

Fortunately, I have managed to track down a number of elderly women who were amongst Alice's earliest pupils, and some of their memoirs are recorded in the following pages. One lady, who particularly comes to mind is Katherine (Kathy) Roberts, (nee Hutchings) now well into her eighties. A most amazing lady of great vitality. Kathy remembers her "Miss Wadland" with great affection, she was a pupil from 1917 to 1924. From some of her stories Kathy obviously enjoyed teasing Alice and some of her impersonations of Alice are absolutely wonderful. One particular impersonation which was hilarious was the way in which "Miss Wadland" would open the door, and walk into the classroom each morning with straight back, erect shoulders and head held high, and say in an authoritative tone "Good morning girls." Kathy went on to say that each morning they would start off with a hymn accompanied by the piano which was played in turn by one of the girls. "Although Miss Wadland was austere, she was very warm underneath, and a perfect lady." Alice's warmth certainly

*Arscotts was previously known as Trevanion House.

41

surfaced when Kathy's father died when she was only aged 12, and Kathy stressed that Alice had shown a lot of kindness to her and her mother during this very difficult time. She continued by saying "Miss Wadland had more of her father's temperament but as the years passed she became sweeter and mellowed more like her mother. Mrs Wadland had a very difficult time with her husband Richard, due to his alcoholism."

"The old Wadland is coming." This is how the village children used to refer to Richard Wadland. He was also known as the "madman" after he had been drinking, which often left him in a bad mood. Richard certainly let the Wadland family down. With his passing in 1916, Alice became the head of the house, even ruling over her mother, but this was protectiveness due to all that her mother had gone through the previous two years and which seemed to shatter most of Eliza's confidence.

Kathy clearly remembers Alice saying that "her girls" were not to play with the village children. I suppose that this would now seem ridiculous, but at the time Alice wanted to groom her young ladies in her own way and not be influenced by the other children. However, it is obvious that Kathy and other pupils took little notice of Alice's request, and went off and met who they wished and did what they wanted. Alice's request was obviously futile and impossible to implement, as most of the pupils were the village children. Nevertheless, Alice's petition did take more effect from the early 1930s when the village was becoming more cosmopolitan, and also with the increasing number of day pupils who travelled to Dolton from various parts of North Devon.

Another of Kathy's memories was when Alice used to put her hands over her face and say despondently, "You will break my heart." Kathy would then reply "But Miss Wadland, your heart was broken years ago" as she used to always say that. Alice certainly left a great impression on Kathy, and even towards the last days of her life, Alice was not afraid of facing death, and Kathy went on to say "she was quite prepared for it as she was so strong in her faith and ready to meet her maker." The following story is Kathy's favourite, and is entitled and told in her own words:

THE CAP & GOWN

"Miss Wadland had a servant called Annie Dymond who was a little simple minded, yet harmless. Annie was the general dogs-body who did all the menial chores around the house. Miss Wadland used to look down on the working classes, and she made it quite clear to Annie that she was to keep her place, and we (the pupils) to ours. In some ways I felt terribly sorry for Annie, as she was always a solitary figure, and now and again I would go up to her and have a chat, much to Annie's reluctance, always on guard worrying that Miss Wadland might appear on the scene.

Anyway, one day we were all in class, sitting around the big table, when Miss Wadland asked us in turn what we would like to do when we left school. All the girls gave Miss Wadland a satisfactory answer until she came to me, and asked "Well Katherine, what would you like to do when you leave school?" To which I replied "I want to be a servant just like Annie, Miss Wadland!" With that Miss Wadland put her hands to her face and said despairingly, "Oh Katherine, you are hopeless." Then I replied "Well that is why I am here Miss Wadland."

∞∞∞∞

Elsie Thomas, 1918 (just 2 terms)

"Whilst I was a boarder at Miss Wadland's, I remember on 11th November rumours going around the village all day, that the Great War had finally ended. Then in the evening, after the boarders (including myself), had gone to bed, Miss Wadland came to wake us up to say that it had just been officially announced in the village that the war was indeed over. So, we had to get out of our beds, get dressed and went off to Dolton church with Miss Wadland for a thanksgiving service."

The Great War had officially ended at 11.00am but it took time for officials to spread the news in rural areas. As Elsie was a boarder, her parents paid 8 guineas a term.

∞∞∞∞

Lilian Jerwood (Chammings), 1920-1928 (approx)

"I was a boarder at Miss Wadland's and I remember her mother, who was a lovely old lady and would read to us until bedtime which was at 8 o'clock."

∞∞∞∞

Irene Lemon, 1917-1919

"Towards the end of my spell at Miss Wadland's, I was introduced to the stories of the ancient Greek myths, and was utterly fascinated. I never really caught up with them again, and when I later did come across them the magic had gone. After leaving Miss Wadland's, I went to the Royal Academy of Music and obtained my L.R.A.M., then returned to it ten years later, as a half-student, and studied the organ under G. D. Cunningham, obtaining my A.R.C.O. I spent all my working life teaching piano and organ privately."

∞∞∞∞

Vera Maynard (Blackmore), 1918-1926

"School started off with a hymn, followed with prayers, and grace was always said before lunch. One of Miss Wadland's favourite countries was Switzerland. She used to come back from her holidays with photos of the Alps, and would talk about them during Geography lessons. I also remember a large map of the world on the wall. School finished at 3.30pm, and we had Friday afternoons off. My parents paid the equivalent of £4.50 a term for my education, and Miss Wadland also taught music after school hours. When we used to work at our sewing or knitting, Miss Wadland would read us stories which included 'Around the World in Eighty Days.' At Christmas, we used to partake in a play or pantomime. One year we enacted 'The Mad Hatters Tea Party.' which was great fun, For this we used Miss Wadland's drawing-room, she would set up the stage, and she did a very good job too. Our parents were invited along to watch the performances. I thought that the 'Alice in

Wonderland' tales were a delight. Concerning lessons, we started French when we were eight, beginning with grammar, and Miss Wadland was keen for us to learn French verbs. Of other memories I can remember Mr Richard Wadland driving through the village like a madman, with his little white pony (welsh cob) and trap. This was when he was a bit drunk, and usually occurred late in the evening."

Vera's family owned the Union Inn which during her child-hood, was a hotel.

∞∞∞

Annie Martin (Elliott), 1917-1919 (approx)

"I was a boarder. Our school uniform comprised of green pinafore dress, camel/green woolly in winter, cream blouse in summer, and we knitted our jumpers! I thought the school was pleasant and peaceful and well organised. Everything that Miss Wadland said was good, she never wasted her words. At one time, I was struggling to read music, I would know the tune but not its name. Miss Wadland quietly closed the music, and said "I can't teach you, you play by ear." We used to go on some nature walks by the river, with the lovely dragonflies and kingfishers. One Christmas we produced the play "Midsummer Night's Dream". The food at school was very good, and beautifully cooked and served. Miss Wadland was so clever and capable, and I appreciated her good example and kindness."

∞∞∞

Phyllis Quick (Folland), 1918-1922/23

"At the age of nine I suffered the trauma of losing my mother during the flu epidemic of 1918. After her death, I went to live with my Grandmother, Mrs Heaman, at Homelea. When she became ill I then became a weekly boarder for a short while, then leaving to join my father at Ashwater, and then going to school in Launceston. At Miss Wadland's I didn't like artichokes, so had to miss my dessert!"

∞∞∞

Mary Squire (Ball), 1917-1919

"Miss Wadland was an excellent teacher, and we all seemed to be happy!"

∞∞∞∞

Nancy Verney (Holwill), 1924-1933

"I remember my first day at school and eating my packed lunch at the table with the boarders, and also Miss Wadland and her mother, who was a very kind and sweet lady. Our uniform consisted of a green gym tunic, cream blouse, brown shoes and green coat."

The school uniform was actually a bottle green colour. Most of Alice's pupils wore some form of uniform but it doesn't appear to have been compulsory. There was also a uniform for boys when they were admitted in Alice's school in 1931.

∞∞∞∞

Ruth Dowding (Arnold), 1927 (just two terms)

"I did indeed go to Miss Wadland's school but I can really remember very little. I think I was there for two terms only, before we left my home at Nethercott, Iddesleigh. I was a weekly boarder at her school. I remember the drive up to the house funnily enough, and the only other things I recall are:

1. Being taught to knit, and knitting a white vest on circular needles!

2. Much enjoying singing the songs from the song book – all the old favourites.

Your relative's education must have been of a high standard, as I had no problem slotting into my age group at Southlands in Exmouth when we moved there."

∞∞∞∞

Another person I had the pleasure of speaking to was Mr Jack Holwill, a great character who remembered Alice well, and had sent his three children to her school. Jack Holwill related many interesting stories to me about Dolton and its people, and the following anecdote.

"Every Monday afternoon at about 4pm, Miss Wadland would either walk or cycle out to Ham Farm (where I lived with my family) and collect her butter, and occasionally she would buy some cream. If Miss Wadland could not come, then she would send one of her pupils.

As a boy I well remember Mr Richard Wadland, who enjoyed his drink a little too much. He used to frequent the Royal Oak. Sadly, Mr Wadland was not a very good example as the Wadlands were a well respected family."

∞∞∞∞

Another memory local people have of Alice is when she was seen during weekdays just after 3.30pm going off on one of her walks with her girl boarders,one behind the other, (known to the boarders as 'crocodile files'). Alice was well known for walking at a good pace, having quite a stride, and at times her boarders had difficulty in keeping up with her.

A DEVON TRAGEDY
MISS FRANCES LUXTON (1908-1975)

To many people locally, and now nationally, Frances Luxton of Winkleigh has become a focus of much intrigue and speculation due to her violent and mysterious death, as well as those of her brothers Robert and Alan in 1975. Frances Luxton was actually a pupil* of Alice, from 1917 to 1924, at Arscotts in Fore Street.

Some of Frances's contemporaries at school remember her as a quiet individual, yet a bright and deeply attentive pupil, and at the same time a reliable friend. I suppose that it was inevitable that a lot of controversy and ill feeling was going to occur when the book 'Earth to Earth' was published.

One point in the book gave a very strong implication that Frances may have had an incestuous relationship with one of her brothers. The idea of this to her contemporaries was utterly repugnant, and without doubt this was a slanderous and hurtful allegation against her good name. The Luxtons were undoubtedly a slightly peculiar family, but perhaps no more so than a lot of other secular rural families of that time, who simply had little to do with the outside world. Various women stated that Frances Luxton was a "devout Christian", even as a girl, she had a very spiritual side to her character. Whilst compiling this book, I also met various people in the Winkleigh district, who knew Frances well, and they also expressed very similar views with regard to Frances's spiritual life. One woman I know called Jean Saunders, knew the Luxtons intimately, and she was absolutely furious and upset by some of the

*For a period Frances was a weekly boarder.

remarks made by the author, and without hesitation she contacted him and made her views quite clear. We all know that a lot of writing is conjectural and it does appear that the author of 'Earth to Earth' slipped up on the particular point mentioned above.

The acquaintance between Alice and Frances started through their parents. The Wadlands, for many decades owned parcels of land in the parish of Winkleigh, and this included about 29 acres of ground (known as Chapple Mill Downs) adjoining West Chapple Farm which was the home of Frances Luxton and her brothers. The Luxtons acquired the land from the Wadlands in the latter part of the 19th century.

THE LUXMOORE ENCOUNTERS

Alocal lady who remembers Alice with respect is Mrs Helen Turrall; her two children Richard and Diane were pupils of Alice but I shall come back to them later. Mrs Turrall related the following story to me.

"In 1917, my parents wanted Miss Wadland to teach my sister, Rosalie Luxmoore, the piano as they had heard of her musical abilities. After being approached, Miss Wadland accepted the request and each Monday after school, Miss Wadland would cycle to our house, Stafford Barton. Rosalie thought a lot of Miss Wadland and always looked forward to her music lessons. I was between four and five years of age at the time, and while the lessons were in progress, I apparently would occasionally appear on the scene. It was mainly inquisitiveness but all the same, I was interrupting them. So Miss Wadland, without fuss would either get me to do some drawing or give me coloured paper and make me cut out letters of the alphabet and stick them onto card. This did the trick in keeping me quiet, and Miss Wadland could resume with her teaching. My sister was aged about eight when she started learning the piano."

When Helen started to learn the piano, she soon proved to have a talent for it and eventually went on to study at the Royal College of Music. One elderly gentleman in the village, a Mr Bert Heard, once said to me that he thought that the two most outstanding personalities in the community had to be Alice Wadland and "Squire" Luxmoore, (Charles Luxmoore) the father of Rosalie. This seemed to be the general opinion in the village and I am also in agreement about Charles Luxmoore; from the stories I have heard about him, he was certainly quite an eccentric. What Alice made of her fellow "personality" is anyone's guess.

Alice's visits to Stafford Barton must have reminded her of her own childhood, as Charles Luxmoore had six daughters, and as the reader will be aware by now, Alice was also one of six girls. The difference was that Charles Luxmoore also had four older sons, opposed to Alice just having one brother. Stafford was always a place full of activity, with the constant liveliness of the Luxmoore girls, though it seems that they were a little more mischievous than the Wadland girls.

Another person who remembered Alice well was a Mrs Olive Hooper, who for some years was in the employment of Alice's aunt Sarah Wadland, and Olive gave the following account.

"Miss Sarah Wadland was a governess of Beaford school, and when I was about to leave school in 1928, she asked my teacher whether there might be anyone who would be interested in going to work for her and her invalid niece Miss Margaret Leverton. My teacher recommended me, and I then got the job. I was paid 4 shillings a week which at the time was a very generous wage.

Sarah Wadland was a very good cook, and she taught me how to cook. She used to enter her dairy produce into county shows, and won a lot of 1st prizes. Sarah Wadland always had to have everything just so, she was a perfectionist.

I was a member of the local Girls' Friendly Society which was organised by Miss Susie Arnold (a friend of Miss Alice Wadland). We usually met on Saturday afternoons, and we had our own little badge which was worn with pride. Every Sunday, Sarah Wadland would prepare to go to Church, so her coachman/handyman (George Madge) would start work and get the horse and coach ready, and off they would go to Beaford Church.

Sarah Wadland was a very good hearted lady, and I think she had much influence over Miss Alice Wadland, and I know that Alice greatly respected her aunt. Alice Wadland and her mother Mrs Eliza Wadland usually came and stayed

51

with Sarah Wadland and Margaret Leverton most week-ends. This was at Southdown, Beaford. It was also traditional that Alice and Eliza came to Southdown on Christmas Day. If any of Alice's sisters were home for the Christmas period, then they would usually come along too. Miss Kathleen Wadland would also visit her aunt and cousin fairly regularly. Miss Winifred Wadland was most pleasant, and she was very much with it, in her dress etc, compared to her sister Alice who was old fashioned in her dress.

Winifred Wadland during most summers, would stay at Westward Ho!, with a Mr Emanuel who was a rather dashing gentleman, and I can remember on one occasion when he visited Southdown, with Miss Winifred, he was wearing long shorts which we local girls quietly had a good titter about. Miss Winifred and Mr Emanuel were at the time living somewhere up country. I can remember Mrs Eliza Wadland spending a lot of time 'tatting', making lace-edgings. My years at Southdown were very happy ones indeed, and I found all the Wadland women very charming, gracious and inspirational."

SAGES
1930 – 1963

The move from Arscotts to Sages, in the summer of 1930, went off smoothly. Again, Alice was then ready for the autumn term. Her years at Sages were to be very happy ones. She rented the property from a Frederick Anstey, a local man. Sages was just perfect for Alice; she had a considerably bigger classroom, could take more boarders, and had a large walled garden which contained the well-known mulberry tree. There was also a large barn behind the property which local tradition says was used as stables for elephants when the circus used to visit Dolton.

To Alice's pupils, it was a place to explore and have fun, with many little nooks and crannies, and small enclosed gardens. The property also had its own tennis court, and this was another star in Alice's book, as she was a very keen tennis player. She encouraged her pupils to play tennis, and she also allowed the people of the parish to make use of the court. When Alice was at Arscotts, many of her former pupils remember playing croquet, and she continued with this when she was at Sages. Apparently, Alice paid a rent of £1.00 a week on the property.

School resumed its normal pace for the next couple of years. Then in 1931, Alice made the decision to accept boys into her school, and the first boy pupil admitted, during the Christmas term, was David Lynch-Blosse, (later Sir David Lynch-Bloss, Bt). David was very much an ordinary boy, and Alice thought him to be a good and bright pupil. However, it was not to be all plain sailing, some of the boys which Alice taught were simply beyond her control, and at times she regretted that she ever accepted them into her school. One person said to me, "Miss Wadland was simply too much of a lady, it wouldn't have hurt if she had given some of the lads a good hiding." With regard to corporal punishment, her limits were either a good smack on the rear, or grabbing a disobedient child by the scruff of the hair, and sending him/her to the corner of the room.

The two most mischievous little rogues that Alice had to put up with were Richard Turrall and Henry Sawrey-Cookson. Most of the time they simply made teaching life very difficult for Alice, so much so, that she called in Richard and Henry's mothers (the fathers were away serving in the war). Alice said quite calmly that Richard and Henry really needed a master. One of the mothers, Mrs Helen Turrall, said "We felt rather guilty about it all, and felt terribly sorry for poor Miss Wadland. She was an extremely tolerant lady, yet even she had her justifiable limits." Ultimately the two boys were sent off to a boys school in Bude, Cornwall, and this in Helen Turrall's view was quite a shock for their system, a place where they did occasionally get a beating. "By her remark that they needed a "master", I thought in other words, they need a good beating." Richard and Henry obviously stand out in many former pupils' minds, as their recurrence is mentioned in some of the following pages. In all fairness to Richard and Henry, they were on the whole just boisterous and cheeky, typical lads. I might add that they have turned out to be two fine and respectable fellows.

With that little episode behind her, Alice continued teaching with a little more normality. Like most teachers, Alice was known to her pupils by various nicknames. She had in fact five nicknames throughout her teaching career in Dolton. The earliest one was "Betty", but I have had trouble in finding out why, or what this stood for. The second was the "Blue Dragon", and the reason for this was that the blue stood for the colours she wore, usually items in navy-blue and of course, I think the "Dragon" is self-explanatory. The third was the "Old Dragon", as many of the children found her age a great mystery. The fourth was "Waddleduck", and the fifth and final nickname was "Miss Waddy". The last two are to do with the 'Wad' bit of her surname, and are all too familiar with me, as I would sometimes be called "Waddle." Occasionally, Alice would, with tongue-in-cheek, call herself the "Old Dragon", but only in front of friends.

The old mulberry tree which is at Sages, was a particular focal point with many of Alice's former pupils. Sadly, some years ago the tree was stuck by lightning, and now only a smaller version remains. However, when I saw the tree for the first time in 1997, I was quite impressed with it. It looked quite healthy, and stands at a height of approximately 30 ft. The original tree was obviously considerably bigger, and during the summer months, it was usually laden with the delicious oblong shaped black fruit and covered with the attractive green foliage. I know that there are those who disagree with me that the fruit is delicious (particularly children), as it is rather an acquired taste. Anyway, there are several stories relating to that old mulberry tree. One was related to me by a number of people who could remember Alice sitting on a little stool underneath the tree reading stories of 'Brer Rabbit', with the children sitting on the ground cross legged.

Another story which a few children well remember concerned Richard Turrell and Henry Sawrey-Cookson. When a lunch hour finished, Alice would usually send a pupil to summon the others back to the classroom, and this was always done with the hand school bell. The child who was asked to undertake this task, usually did it with great importance and gusto, making a very loud noise. Anyway, back to the story, when the child had summoned the others, they all filed back into the classroom, that is except Richard and Henry. Alice was not the least surprised and went out and scoured the premises calling for the boys. Where do you think they were hiding? Yes, up in the mulberry tree, the one place that Alice never thought of looking. While Alice was scouring the place, and becoming more infuriated, Richard and Henry got a little bored with their trick, climbed down from their hideaway and headed back to the classroom. Alice in the meantime was virtually beside herself, and decided to give up the hunt. She in turn headed back to the classroom feeling totally frustrated yet also rather anxious as to what had happened to them, or what they were up to elsewhere. She also thought that her appearance in the class would rest her mind and keep the other pupils in check just in case they had any ideas of getting up to any antics. Upon entering the classroom, she immediately viewed Richard and Henry, who sat there looking totally angelic, as if nothing had happened. When she roared their names, they both replied in such sweet and innocent voices, "Yes Miss Wadland?" What little darlings!

At times, Alice certainly deserved her well-earned breaks and as usual she would head off to the continent with Kathleen. However, in 1934, Alice and Kathleen decided to have a quieter holiday in the UK, and their chosen destination was 'Bexhill Holiday Fellowship Camp', in East Sussex. This was a centre for Christians, with all sorts of recreational activities, but a place that was very much geared towards forms of worship and those who required solitude. Alice and Kathleen returned to this favoured place on further occasions.

WAR, EVACUEES AND A DEATH
1939-1945

Like all communities, the outbreak of World War II enveloped another turbulent time for many Doltonians. However, Alice continued with her teaching which was clearly a necessity. The only way in which this war effected Alice was an influx of extra pupils into her school, mainly evacuees from London. Most of the children who arrived in Dolton soon settled into their new surroundings, which to them, was like heaven on earth. Any large houses in the parish took in evacuees, including some of the farming families. Some of the evacuee children who went to Alice's were there for no more than a month or so, some stayed on for perhaps two or three years. The war inflicted many uncertainties and those who had to leave at short notice found it a grievous wrench, yet their memories of Dolton and its people would be embedded into their minds for the rest of their days. Indeed a number have returned over the years. Thankfully, the evacuee children soon integrated and formed close bonds with Alice's other pupils, although by the 1940s the school was already very cosmopolitan. For the rest of the war period, the school continued without any major interruptions. The only thing that was an upset for Alice was the death of her mother Eliza which occurred on the 30th of December 1944 at the age of 86.

For the last couple of years of her life, Eliza had become virtually bedridden, but as usual, Alice always took the greatest of care of her mother. Even during her last years Eliza remained cheerful, good humoured, always the optimist, and her inner warmth at once radiated and touched anyone who came into her presence, whereupon they would become inseparable. She certainly knew how an individual ticked, and she had the ability of melting the coldest heart. Several of Alice's former pupils remember her with much affection. Perhaps her abilities were from the days when, before her marriage to Richard, she was also a teacher. Little is known about her career, although it is known that for some years (c.1881), she was a governess to the children of a Helen Ley in Bideford. Eliza simply abounded in humanity and tolerance and she would strive to bring out the best in an individual, even those who were regarded by society as 'no-hopers' or the 'dredges' of humanity. She believed in giving everyone a chance. She died peacefully, strong in her faith, and reassured that her daughters had all developed good careers.

∞∞∞

During the 1940s the school saw a flow of children from interesting families, this included Simon Whistler, the son of Laurence Whistler the well known poet, writer and glass engraver, and his mother Jill (Furse), the beautiful actress who tragically died in 1943 at her home of Venton. Simon then went on to Stowe, and then the Royal Academy of Music, and is now an accomplished musician, and like his father, a glass engraver.

Another former pupil with an interesting background was Anthony Haden-Guest, the son of Lord Peter Haden-Guest who was connected with the United Nations. Anthony now lives in New York and is a successful writer and international correspondent. There was also Christopher Ommanney, who was a member of a prominent family deeply ingrained in the maritime world which included a good sprinkling of Admirals as well as their equals on land, ie Generals. One of Christopher's most well known and greatly respected 20th century relatives was Francis Downes Ommanney, the authoritative oceanographer, who had written several books. Christopher's family was also related to the Luxmoores of

Stafford Barton, as Rosalie Maud Ackworth Luxmoore (wife of Charles Luxmoore) was an Ommanney by birth, and very proud of her oceanic ancestry. One of Rosalie's favourite sayings was, "the Ommanneys stink of the sea!"

∞∞∞

Another major event which was to effect Alice during the 1940s was the radical education act of 1944 which became law on the 3rd of August. It witnessed the introduction of a series of important measures of 'social reconstruction'. The bill was passed through parliament by Mr R. A. Butler, who was the principal author of the act and who at that time was President of the Board of Education. The Act eventually became known as the Butler Act. Passing successfully through parliament, and with Royal Assent, it was said that "to make it a real success the full cooperation of every citizen is required." Many of the Act's fundamentals are still in effect here in the closing stages of the 20th century.

The act was arranged in five parts containing one hundred and twenty-two sections, or clauses as they were often called, and nine schedules. The schedules dealt in detail with matters occurring out of various clauses. The part which was of relevance to Alice and her school was Part III (Sections 70-75), dealing with independent/private schools. Alice saw some of the new measures of the Act as infringements, interfering with her preferred methods of teaching and the way in which she administered her establishment. Alice also had to endure more visitations of educational inspectors (appointed by the Minister of H. M. Government), who in her opinion were nothing more than vexing bureaucrats, and usually on an initial meeting Alice was rather frosty. Even an inspector would tread lightly, soon realising that Alice had quite a presence and she could have an unnerving effect on an individual. Alice met most of the new criteria: a publication by H. C. Dent, entitled 'The Education Act 1944' (published just after the act became law), quoted and stated the following which concerned Part III of Independent Schools:

When I have been explaining the provisions of the Education Act, 1944, somebody has always asked 'what is the position of the private school?' Sections 70-75 answer that question.

The Minister shall appoint one of his officers to be Registrar of Independent (private) schools; and it shall be the duty of the Registrar of Independent schools to keep a register of all Independent Schools which shall be open to public inspection at all reasonable times.

The proprietor of any private school may make application to be registered. The registration will be provisional until the school has been inspected on behalf of the Minister, who will then confirm it (provided of course that the report on the school is satisfactory). If the Minister's satisfied in respect of any school or class of schools that this procedure is unnecessary, the school or schools will be exempted from it and become automatically registered (Section 70).

There was considerable dissatisfaction in Parliament about this last provision which, it was alleged, smacked of favouritism. Mr Butler explained that it was simply meant to save trouble. The Ministry, he said, would have quite enough to do inspecting schools about which they knew nothing, without adding to their work by inspecting schools they already knew (by previous inspection) to be thoroughly efficient.

There are four grounds upon which a school may be refused registration or removed from the register. These are:

a) That the school premises or any parts thereof are unsuitable for a school.

b) that the accommodation provided at the school premises is inadequate or unsuitable, having regard to the numbers, ages and sex of the pupils attending the school.

c) That efficient and suitable instruction is not being provided, having regard to the ages and sex of the pupils.

d) That the proprietor of the school or any teacher employed therein is not a proper person to be proprietor or to be a teacher in any school (Section 71).

A school would not immediately be struck off the register. The procedure is that the Minister serves upon the proprietor a "notice of complaint", and unless the matter complained of is deemed by the Minister to be irremediable, the proprietor is given not less than six months to put it right (Section 71).

The proprietor may appeal by referring the complaint to an Independent Schools Tribunal to be set up under the Act (Section 72). The Sixth Schedule provides that this tribunal shall consist of two panels to be appointed by the Lord Chancellor, (the "legal panel") and the Lord President of the Council, (the "educational panel") respectively. Members appointed to either panel must have appropriate qualifications. Any appeal will be determined by a tribunal of three persons from these panels, a chairman from the legal panel, and two members from the educational panel. The decision of the tribunal is final.

From six months after the coming into operation of this Part of the Act, any person conducting an unregistered school, or who, being disqualified from acting as a teacher, accepts or endeavours to obtain employment in any school, will be liable, for a first offence, to a fine not exceeding £20, for a second or subsequent offence to a fine not exceeding £50 or up to three months imprisonment, or both (Section 73). Any person disqualified by an order made under the Education (Scotland) Act 1945, is thereby disqualified also under the Education Act 1944 (Education Act 1946, Second Schedule).

A disqualified person may apply to the Minister to have his disqualification removed, and if his application is refused may appeal to the Independent Schools tribunal (Section 74).

Part III of the Act will come into operation on the date to be appointed by the Order in Council.

JOSEPH PATERSON LUSK, M.C., M.B., Ch.B.

One annual visitor to the school was Dr Lusk (a Scotsman), who would undertake a medical check on the pupils, most of whom dreaded being in his presence. Lusk was a rather aggressive character who was formerly an army doctor. When he moved to Dolton in 1920, he resided at the Union Hotel, renting some rooms from the Palmers who were the landlords. It was not just the pupils who dreaded being in his company, but also most of the grown-ups; a fellow who showed little sympathy towards his patients, always shouting and swearing and rambling on, lecturing individuals on how they should lead their lives.

Ironically, for all his pontificating, he was apparently once out on a late night call at Locks Hill Cottage, when enroute he stumbled, falling into a hedge which resulted in a nasty gash across his nose. The following day he was sent to Exeter where he received medical attention, but afterwards he neglected his condition and a couple of weeks after the accident he died of lockjaw. It doesn't sound as if the majority of the community were particularly saddened by his demise. As one local lady said, "he was probably an excellent army doctor, but he had little tact or understanding when dealing with civilians."

Even Alice found him a rather abrasive figure, and on one or two occasions he was known to get a little cross with the pupils. However, Alice would soon come to their defence like a protective hen with her chicks, and would curtly remind Lusk that whilst in her school, he was to conduct himself in a cordial manner. No doubt Lusk probably found Alice quite a formidable character. If cornered, Alice could prove to be a lady that you did not cross swords with. The one person who could mellow and humour the doctor was Alice's mother, who would on occasion entertain him for afternoon tea.

∞∞∞∞

The school routine during the latter part of the 1940s and 1950s stayed very much the same as it had when Alice first established the school during the 1st World War. There were some progressive changes, including the introduction of milk during the 1940s. At 11.00 a.m. each school morning, every child was given a 1/3 pint of bottled milk. It was something that the majority of the children enjoyed, particularly during the summer months, but they were not quite so keen on having to consume it during cold winter months, especially if the crate of milk had been sitting outside the door a little too long. As usual, the school morning always started off with hymns and prayers.

Alice never liked to see her pupils idle, whether in class or outside during their breaks. One of her frequent sayings was "the Devil makes work for idle hands." If she saw a child kicking about aimlessly she would soon get them doing something to occupy their minds, even to the point of telling them what games to play. Even during the lunch break when they were all sitting around the table, Alice would not let the children remain idle. She would make the pupils recite the capitals of the world and on what rivers they stood. She certainly believed in perseverance, knowing that it would always pay off; many of her former pupils will vouch for that.

If a child had difficulty in a certain subject, and then said "Miss Wadland, I can't do this!" She would fold her arms, head held high, with eyes closed, and say quite firmly "Yes you can do it, there is no such word as can't." Without doubt Alice had the right attitude and she helped many children overcome their difficulties. In everything she did with her pupils she was a confidence builder. When Alice was in front of her pupils in class, she was always very formal, rarely ever showing her emotions. Yet,as I have already said, she did have a wonderful sense of humour. She would never tolerate any deliberate nonsense from her pupils, however if a child did make a mistake, or a light joke, she would still keep a straight face, but there were moments when she would cover her face with a hand to hide any sign of amusement. There was the odd occasion when she just could not contain herself, almost bursting with laughter which usually resulted in a quick exit from the classroom, making sure that the door was firmly closed behind her. Again, it is nice to know that she was only human and not always austere and without compassion as some people thought.

∞∞∞∞

Joyce Arnold (Chammings) 1924-1933

"I was a boarder at Miss Wadland's and in my opinion she was an exceptional lady. I know she kept home for her mother. She sadly suffered the loss of some male relatives during the 1914-18 war. I can remember going to 'blow' the bellows of the church organ when she was practising for the Sunday service at Dolton Church. The practice usually took place on a Thursday evening. Both Mrs & Miss Wadland were very kind to me during the years that I was their only boarder. I went home on Friday after lunch, and returned on Monday in time for school at 9 am. The weeks were always full of interest for me, particularly as the Wadlands had a good library, and I became an avid reader, something that has remained with me to this day. I remember that some years Miss Wadland went to Switzerland during the summer holidays and we used to hear about the countryside and her holiday adventures. To me it was another world away from my farming background. She was a strict disciplinarian but she was at the same time very fair. I remember marching to the War Memorial for the service on the 11th of November each year. We used to go for a walk everyday, two to three miles usually, and we used to play tennis and croquet. I enjoyed all the lessons except for French. Miss Wadland taught me to be practical, to work hard, and also to be interested in politics and in European history."

∞∞∞∞

64

May Gilder (Bailey) 1925-1936

"Miss Wadland was a strict teacher but greatly respected. She believed in the 3Rs (Reading, Writing and Arithmetic) as well as History, Geography, French, Art and Needlework which Mrs Wadland helped with."

Indeed, Alice strongly believed in the 3Rs. She was adamant that they were the first three most important approaches to education. Most of her pupils supported her views on this particular issue, expressing that the 3Rs were of great benefit to them, and that not enough emphasis on these three categories is in present-day education. As I am from a younger generation I was quite surprised how strongly people felt about this particular issue.

∞∞∞

Moira E Couper (Hunt), 1938-1940

"I must tell you the significance of my experience at Miss Wadland's school of which I have only recently become aware. I remember well the room, and the large table covered with a heavy green cloth, around which all the pupils sat. It was so different from other schools I had attended where we were all seated in individual desks facing the front and the teacher. I can remember feeling very comfortable with this new method of seating, and how I enjoyed the interaction with others, and Miss Wadland."

∞∞∞

Sylvia Sullivan-Tailyour (Lynch-Blosse), 1934-1941

"I am delighted that at long last "Miss Wadland", as she will always be to me, is getting recognition for the very fine work she did with so many young people, in giving them a really sound grounding in so many facets of their formal education. When I went away to school in 1942, a school with a very high academic reputation, I was well up to and beyond standard in most subjects, and even if it was me who "broke her

heart", I did eventually attain university, mainly due to her excellent grounding! I am sure that all her past students will remember her as I do, with great affection. She was always fair, very strict, but immensely kind, and only in real desperation did she ever stamp her foot when we really deserved to have our necks wrung! You may or may not know that in the early forties there was a gentleman who tried to court Miss Wadland. His name was Mr John Snell. She found him very tiresome I think as he would appear at the school window with large bunches of flowers for her, and wouldn't go away, which embarrassed Miss Wadland acutely! I think he was a bit odd! Eventually she had to lock the garden door against him. Another memory which particularly comes to mind, is returning to school on the afternoon of Dunkirk, all of us very tired, upset and quiet, and we said prayers for everyone's safety. I also remember Mrs Wadland, a splendid old lady, with a really naughty sense of humour, and considerably less straight than her daughter."

∞∞∞∞

I did enjoy reading Sylvia's contribution. Alice certainly comes across as a lady who enjoys life, and from reading some of the other little anecdotes, she had quite a sense of humour too. In fact, I have already found out quite a lot about John Snell, from earlier pupils. He was a harmless enough character, perhaps a fractionally eccentric. He was a prosperous farmer who lived at Little Cudworthy in the parish. John Snell did indeed have a fondness for Alice but it's obvious that Alice repelled his advances. In her part, Alice no doubt respected him but it is almost certain that she made it quite clear to John that their acquaintance was to remain on a purely platonic basis. As I have mentioned before, Alice had made it quite clear from the start that she wanted to commit her life purely to teaching. Simply, she was a workaholic, or should I say a teachaholic! However, it appears that John Snell took little notice of Alice's protestations. A few years ago I met Vida Folland who was a housekeeper for John Snell at Little Cudworthy. We had an interesting conversation, and she gave me the following account:

"Every Friday afternoon, I knew what was going to happen. Mr Snell would clean up, put on his suit and bow tie, and then head off for Dolton to see Miss Wadland. Of course he knew that the school was closed on Friday afternoons. It was all very funny." Vida went on to say *"towards the last years of John Snell's life it became difficult to look after him, and whenever I saw Miss Wadland in the village, she would always asked how I was coping, as she thought I looked strained. She was always considerate."*

From some of the other accounts, it appears that John Snell had one favourite bow tie – which was red. Also, it was not only Friday afternoon when he would try and see Alice, as some pupils distinctly remember him appearing outside the classroom window, usually with a large bunch of flowers. Alice and John Snell's acquaintance started when John employed Alice to do his farm accounts. Alice had worked on John's accounts for several years. I think John Snell remained hopeful to the end, that perhaps one day Alice would change her mind but it wasn't to be. He died on the 29th of September 1944. He had appointed Alice and Frederick Anstey to be his executors, and in his Will he bequeathed the generous amount of £1000 to Alice. It seems that John Snell was a very thoughtful and charitable gentleman as he made several bequests in his will.

∞∞∞

Jean Lock (Heal), 1940-1943

"When I went to Alice's school, we use to carry a packed lunch etc, and we ate around the same table with her and her mother, "the maid" in uniform, would bring in their cooked lunch and we would have a pot of tea and plates to put our food on. This table that we sat around was mahogany, about 12ft x 6ft, and this was also where we did our lessons. Mrs Eliza Wadland was a very cheerful old lady, not as stern as Alice, she used to put quizzes to us – Guess lighting-up times etc! Most amusing she was, Eliza 5ft tall and Alice 5ft 9ins. There was quite a good size

The original timetable (above) was kindly given by Jean Hockin (now Mrs Elliot), and the copy (below) gives a translation.

Pupil: Joan Hockin   __Time Table__   **September 1940**

Monday	Tuesday	Wednesday	Thursday	Friday
French: Conversation. Scripture: Old Testament. Geography: British Isles. Algebra. Arithmetic. Mapping. Nature Study or Composition.	Singing. French: Grammar. French: Verbs. History. Algebra. Needlework.	Reading. French: Translation. English: Dictation. Spellings. Poetry. Drawing.	Singing. Scripture: New Testament. Arithmetic. History. Geometry.	French: Conversation. Arithmetic. Geography. Literature. General Knowledge. Darwing.

68

fireplace in the room, and Alice always kept a couple of fire bricks in the side of it, so that it only burnt one log at a time, rather cold in the worst winter days! We had to stack our books tidily in marked places on shelves when we finished lessons each day. One pupil had a special wooden (coveted) box! We always had an hour's homework, and we had to walk three miles to our home across fields after 3.45 p.m. In the winter, it would be getting dark when we reached home. My father drove us in the car on some mornings, from Cudworthy. My cousin Joan Hockin lived with us and used to school with us, as her father refused to send her to the then 'New Torrington Secondary School' because it was war-time, and the school was built of a lot of glass! We had no milk at school as it was war-time. Alice would quote a great deal from Shakespeare, the Bible and various famous poets. When we were allowed on rare occasions to go into the garden, we liked to stand under a huge mulberry tree, and then got into trouble for mulberry stains on our shoes. Alice Wadland was a genius, she could do any mortal thing! Carve wood, cook, as well as all the subjects she taught. A great disciplinarian which meant work, work, work, no time for pleasure or frivolities. I only wished that I had longer with her. Her knowledge was extensive."

∞∞∞∞

Diane Joynson (Turrall), 1941-1944

"I remember on one occasion playing under the mulberry tree, and then falling down, my dress covered with juice. In class we used to sit around a large table which was covered with a large green blanket. I also remember the naughtiness of my brother Richard, and cousin Henry Sawrey-Cookson, who were always up to something, and were in the end taken away to go to Prep School – poor Miss Wadland."

∞∞∞∞

Isabel Trewin (Heal), 1941-1947

"Lessons at Sages were conducted around a large dining table which was cleared at lunch times and laid with a white damask table cloth, cutlery and silver serviette rings for Mrs Wadland, Miss Wadland and boarders (if any). Children who were day pupils brought a packed lunch, and sat at the same table. Mrs Wadland once said "Digestion starts in the mouth, so masticate your food well." This 'new' word masticate made a great impression on me as I was only aged six. Mrs Wadland used to wear black crepe dresses, with lace trimmings. She had beautiful table manners which she tried to instill in us. After lunch we had to lie on the floor for five minutes to help our digestion. Miss Wadland was nicknamed 'Waddy', but no one called her this to her face as she was quite a formidable woman. For many years she was the organist at St Edmonds, Dolton, and taught the Bible at school more thoroughly that any priest I have met. She read the Times, and also enjoyed Punch magazine, often reading out useful or amusing items to us over lunch. We sometimes had physical education on the lawn at the back of the house under the mulberry tree. We used to also play croquet. Crocuses grew in the lawn at the front of Sages, which were picked and used for drawing lessons; a spray of holly and berries was another favourite, and also rose-hips. I remember wisteria growing along the verandah at the front of the house. We used to pick the mulberries, putting them into our breast pockets, and would end up with stained blouses. Another memorable thing was the day when Cissie Holwill picked some gooseberries from the garden and hid them in her pocket. When she pulled out her handkerchief in class, the gooseberries flew far and wide. Miss Wadland was not amused but we all thought it was hilarious. Finally, I remember Miss Wadland saying "treat your voice as an instrument that you have with you always." She was referring to the singing voice."

∞∞∞∞

Richard Turrall, 1943-1945

"I remember "Miss Wadland's" only as a kindergarten, and I attended it for two years before going to my prep school (St Peter's, Bude) at seven years old. My cousin and I were sent to Miss Wadland's by our mothers out of desperation rather than for more altruistic reasons, to start our education. We were both fatherless, since both his and mine had been abroad since about 1941, and the mothers had to do their best on their own. We were almost entirely out of control and had experienced little or no discipline. Miss Wadland I suppose was deputed to instill some, but she fared no better. I remember spending much time out of the classroom, having been ordered by Miss Wadland to "go out of the door." Henry's place was 'the corner' (of the room), and he spent about as many hours in his place as I did in mine. I remember once being sent out of the room, and being of a curious nature, picking up a china jug on the hall table. To my absolute astonishment and terror, the thing started to play music, which only stopped on being returned to its place. This was the only time I remember being frightened, not having the wit to work out how a musical jug functioned. I imagined the place haunted, and probably behaved for a whole week, rather than again find myself in the presence of the jug! Finally, I remember being very fond of Miss Wadland, and I think I might have started to learn something from her eventually. However, I believe she asked my mother to remove me, and Henry and I found ourselves in a rather different environment at Bude. There the response to ill behaviour was six of the best, and I made a start to settle down and work."

ooooooo

Henry Sawrey-Cookson, 1942-1944

"I was at the school from about the age of three and a half to four and three-quarters, and was eventually expelled as Miss Wadland could not control some of us boys! I was once caught in Miss Wadland's bedroom, dressing up in her underwear. On another occasion, I fell from a tree into her cucumber frames."

∞∞∞∞

Joan Elliott, (Hockin), 1940-1942

"I was always happy at school. We were all helped individually, until Miss Wadland was satisfied that the standard required was reached. I just praise Miss Wadland, and her method of teaching."

Roger Page, 1942-1945

"The school during my time was at Sages. We had to walk along the side entrance to the back door, where we changed into house shoes, our outdoor shoes being placed in a rack. We then walked down a corridor to the schoolroom which had French windows looking out over the front garden. This we did not use. Inside the schoolroom was a large table covered with a green baize cloth. There was a smaller table at the top end where the younger children sat with Miss Wadland at the head, and the older children sat round the big table, at the french window end. We were allotted tasks, and we got on with them quietly and conscientiously. My first task was copying pothooks and stokes which were gradually developed into letters. I remember learning to read and write in a very short space of time, but if one's writing got careless, it was back to pothooks and strokes. I should be doing nothing else now! The break for milk was spent, weather permitting, in the back garden, which contained a bit of a lawn and a large mulberry tree. For painting, a favourite subject was rose-hips. Any student of Miss Wadland's will tell you that when painting these in red, you should always leave a spot in the middle where the white paper showed through – the highlight– to omit this step was one of the worst crimes you could commit. Although I was too young to learn French, I well remember French records (speech) being played on an old wind-up gramophone, to aid the pronunciation. Discipline worked very well until the arrival of Richard Turrall, who would not conform. He would get up from his chair without permission and wander around the room, even interfering with other children who were trying to work. For punishment he was sent out of the room,

where he made further nuisance of himself by chiming the fish bowl which stood in the corridor. He also took the key of the old clock that stood in the hall, and hid it. It was never recovered! Years later when Miss Wadland asked him what he had done with it he couldn't remember.

Miss Wadland took history and geography seriously. For history, I remember a yellow book with black outlined figures on it. We started with the Ancient Britons and Roman, Saxons, Norman Kings and Plantagenets. No doubt we would have gone further but the war ended and, I was aged eight, my family moved to America. For geography we learnt that there were six continents, including 'North-and-South-America' This caused me great trouble at school in America, where it was claimed that there were six continents. When I left Miss Wadland's school I had a good idea of the shape of the world, the oceans, continents, major rivers, mountains, deserts, and which parts of the map were pink. As was usual at that time, we learnt our multiplication tables by heart. Miss Wadland used the method of competition a great deal, standing us in a line. If we could answer a question that the person above us could not, then we moved up one place. This method was used for our tables, spelling, history and geography.

I was very happy at Miss Wadland's, she was an excellent teacher. My wife and I visited her on one occasion, probably about a year before her death. It was a warm sunny day, and she gave us coffee on the lawn. Her sister was also there. She showed me the old history books and all the other books she had used, and she gave me one of the old paint palettes as a souvenir. At that time, she told me that she had taught over three hundred children.

∞∞∞∞

John Heal, 1942-1947

"I remember Mrs Eliza Wadland used to come in and have lunch with us all. Mrs Wadland was very good at conversing with the pupils, and she had quite a sense of humour. We used to take our own packed lunch but were supplied with jugs of water. When we were doing arithmetic, we had a jotting pad in which we worked out our sums in rough. Once these were completed, we then transferred them to our good exercise book, as the sums had to be all precisely written out. If a child could not do something in a particular subject, Miss Wadland would lay it in, and start stamping her finger on the table saying "I just have to keep on keeping on." Then she would go on to say "Why can't you do it?" She would then refer to some former pupil who could do it. She would persevere with us until we got it right. In her own way she was showing us that anything was possible. If Miss Wadland found something rather funny she would make up an excuse to leave the classroom for a few minutes. Some of us in the class knew very well that she was probably having a good laugh. However, once she came back into the room she was her formal self. Once I was instructed to do a sum, and after I had finished working it out, Miss Wadland came over, only to tell me that I had done it wrong. I said that I just could not see it. She then started laying into me saying "What do you mean? Of course you can do it!" I then said "I can't." She showed me how to do the sum, and sure enough she arrived at the same figure as myself. This got her into quite a flap. She tried it again and still it worked out the same. However, it was soon discovered that the sum in the text book was printed incorrectly. Miss Wadland wrote a sharp letter to the publishers of the book. When the publishers replied, Miss Wadland told me that they had apologised for any inconvenience caused. However, Miss Wadland was in no way going to apologise to me!"

∞∞∞∞

Georgina Elstone (Molland), 1940-1942

"I was a boarder at Miss Wadland's, and each morning at 11.00 am we would stop for a break, the boarders were usually given a piece of dough cake and a hot drink. Miss Wadland used to have her own maid who also cooked lunch for the boarders. Miss Wadland would sit as usual at the head of the table. After we had eaten our main course, she would ring a small bell, letting the maid know that we were ready for the dessert. I remember the time when my father was late in getting my sister and I to school one Monday morning. When we did eventually arrive, we went straight up to our bedroom to leave our luggage there. Then as we descended the stairs, Monica (my sister) dropped her pencil case which made quite a din falling down the staircase. On hearing the noise, Miss Wadland came rushing out of the classroom saying "Are you alright mother?", only to find much to her relief that it was only us girls. About this time Mrs Wadland was beginning to fail, and Miss Wadland was always concerned about her. After school finished each day, Miss Wadland would send the boarders out for a walk which lasted for about an hour. The day ended with us (the boarders) going to bed about 9 p.m."

∞∞∞

Audrey Ridif (Ford), 1943-1949

"I remember her as being very strict, unbending and unapproachable as far as the younger pupils were concerned, although she taught basic skills well. There were certain people who were Miss Wadland's favourites. She liked people with money and title."

∞∞∞

I think that Audrey's view concerning Alice's like for money was a little uncharitable. Admittedly, Alice was shrewd with her finances, but she could never be accused of being a money grabber. We also have to bear in mind that her shrewdness was a benefit, as she took running her school most seriously, and being a private concern, she certainly had no peace of mind about having any funding from the educational authority. There were times when the class size decreased considerably, and Alice had to budget on a shoestring. Several former pupils have said that their parents often remarked how cheap it was to send their children to her school, and it was wondered how she made herself a decent living.* Simply, Alice taught for the love of it, her

*Alice's personal circumstances were reasonably secure, as she had some investments in stocks and shares, income from a property which she let, and a share of income from tenanted properties, in Roborough village.

75

life was teaching – absolute commitment, and the hope of contributing to the betterment of mankind. Money was not her goal, and she was definitely no glutinous materialist.

Alice was never one to waste anything. She couldn't bear seeing unnecessary extravagance, probably reflecting on her father's frivolousness and living through two world wars. At times her economical habits were perhaps a little too ridiculous. I remember Kath Harris telling me a humorous anecdote about how on one occasion she and her husband Len gave Alice a lift into town. En-route, whilst discussing what shopping was needed, Alice and Kath got onto the subject of toilet paper. Alice said that she didn't like 'Andrex' as she found it far too thin, and that when she did have to use it, she she had to use not one, but two squares at a time (which Alice obviously regarded as lavishness). Kath thought Alice's comments were absolutely hilarious, but immediately suppressed her amusement when she realised that Alice said it with such seriousness. I can only conclude that Alice's frugality was at times beyond the pale!

ᴔᴔᴔᴔᴔ

Siôn Silyn-Roberts, 1943-1944

"My recollection is that for the short period I was in Dolton, I was very much the hopeless case at the school. She probably regarded me as a visitor. I can remember only sitting at a long table at the right hand side of the end furthest from the window, with about twelve other children. Miss Wadland, I think we nicknamed her 'Waddy', sat at the other end with the light behind her so I only saw her face when she came down to admonish me for what ever crime I had committed that had drawn her attention to me. There was a girl called Rachel, who would now be delighted to know that the only reason I remember her is that she chewed her eraser! I can remember two other tales from that period because they were repeated to me later. The vicar came to visit us at Brook Cottage, and found only Roger Page and I. He asked where our mothers were, and we told him "the pub". We were not very popular, and I

have wondered how many mothers came to hear of that. We also told the vicar that we were brothers, and that I was six months older than Roger, so we can't have had too much credibility!"

∞∞∞∞∞

Ruth Jones (Lendon), 1944-1947

"Mr Wadland, your letter indeed seemed an echo from the past. For me it stirred up memories I really would like to forget. I'm afraid I was not Miss Wadland's favourite pupil by any means. I was a total rebel, and all my memories of Miss Wadland are of her face registering either disapproval or despair about my work or behaviour. I really felt that when I left in 1947, she was glad to see the back of me. I always meant to return and apologise for giving her such a headache. I too became a teacher, and head of department, and really am quite a sober and law abiding citizen, something I know Miss Wadland could never envisage. One thing of interest I'm sure you would like to know, is that I rode my pony to school every day and left him in a loose box in the farm adjoining the school."

∞∞∞∞∞

Ann Blakely (Hopper), 1946-1947

"My brother and I both joined Miss Wadland's school in January 1946. She schooled me for a scholarship at Edgehill College in Bideford, which I won and then I went there in the autumn of 1947. Miss Wadland was an excellent teacher which even I realised, and though I was her pupil for such a short length of time, I was a complete year ahead of other pupils at Edgehill. Unfortunately, I wasted my first year at Edgehill, and never really reached my potential afterwards. My memories of Miss Wadland are that she was very strict, yet fair. My brother gave her a rough time but I don't really know what he did. We also did singing, and being told to keep our heads up high, and hold the hymn/song books up so we could see, but low enough that

77

our voices projected over the top of the book. I often think of that. Behind her back, and even now we referred to your cousin as 'Waddy', or sometimes 'Miss Waddy', but never having written it down before, have no idea whether it should be spelt with a 'y' or an 'ie'. However it was spelt, she was a great lady that I remember with affection. Wish I could have been with her longer."

∞∞∞

Simon Whistler, 1947-1949

"My memories for that period are very hazy, but I do remember walking two miles each way in all weathers across the fields from Halsdon. This is as sharp a memory as anything that happened at school! The only other thing that I can remember is the mulberry tree in the garden."

∞∞∞

Mildred Down (Heard), 1940-1943

"I remember sometimes that we were allowed to play in the back garden. When the school bell rang, we headed back to the classroom, but we had to change out of our outdoor shoes, leave them on a ledge in the porch, and then put on out indoor shoes. After school hours Miss Wadland also taught me the piano at a guinea a term."

∞∞∞

Nicholas West, 1948-1952

"I remember distinctly Miss Wadland announcing the death of King George VI – the oil lamps were lit; a cold February afternoon."

∞∞∞

Of all the pupils that took the eleven plus exam, only one child failed, much to Alice's annoyance. In her eyes, even one failure was regarded as being an ill reflection on her school, and would tarnish her reputation beyond repair. There is actually a rather comical story relating to the poor child who failed the eleven plus exam, but I have omitted all names involved out of decency.

The story was related to me by a woman, who also had a child at the school, about the same time as the child mentioned above. Anyway, one day the mother of the child who failed the exam, and the other woman and her child were all going off together, on the bus to the local town of Great Torrington. The bus was full of passengers and during the journey the two mothers sat next to each other, and their children sat in a seat in front of them.

The conversation turned to school, and the mother of the unfortunate child started saying how well her child was doing at "Miss Wadland's" and how she thought that she would do very well in the forthcoming eleven plus exam. On hearing that, the child of the other mother turned around and said in a very loud voice, "Huh! you must be joking! I heard Miss Wadland say the other day that if she gets your daughter through the eleven plus it will be a miracle." Suddenly there was total silence on the bus, the mother of the unfortunate child was totally deflated, and sat there agape. The other mother said that she was so embarrassed, and that she felt like strangling her child, who in the meantime had turned around and continued her conversation with the unfortunate child as if nothing had happened. The mother went on to say to me that she felt like crawling under one of the bus seats. The result from this was that for a time, the relationship between the mothers was strained, yet the children continued to be good friends. As the mother concluded to me, "the innocent always suffer!"

∞∞∞∞

David Willis, 1957-1959

"While my father served his last two years in Germany, my mother moved with my elder brother and I to Dolton. There she rented Rose Cottage from Miss Wadland. My brother, then nearly seventeen, went to Plymouth College. I was nearly five. My mother chose to send me to Miss Wadland's school and so we visited it before term started. Miss Wadland offered us tea and we sat in the top right hand corner of the classroom, in front of the alphabet chart. I remember that the back of the chart was covered in pictures of goldfish. My first few lessons were devoted to drawing pothooks, to develop a rounded writing style. There were two other children doing similar work. We would each be called up to read to Miss Wadland as she sat in the top left hand corner of the room, to the left of the door. If our reading, or any other work, showed lack of effort we would be sent to stand in the corner of the room. More serious errors were dealt with by dismissal from the room, to sit on a bench in a dark corridor at the back of the house. I remember this happening to me on at least two occasions. Once I shared the bench with a particularly odious boy aged about ten. On another occasion I had been left alone for so long that I assumed I had been forgotten and wandered home. Nothing was ever said about this, so my assumption may have been correct. Occasionally we had a fire practice, however we younger ones never really understood whether there was actually a fire or not. At break time we went to an area of concrete and shrubs where we played organised conventional games such as 'Oranges and Lemons'.

I know that Miss Wadland was a kindly woman but I rather feared her. Her high cheek bones (smooth and rosy), seemed one minute to be smiling, the next to be scolding. There were twelve or fourteen of us, the elder children sitting at the end of the table by the window at the front of the house; the youngest sitting at the end nearest the door. We were all kept busy but if there were distractions they were generally beneficial. I would overhear the exciting history stories being taught to my left or some complicated sum being solved for the boy across the table. I left school when we moved (temporarily) to London two years later. However we often returned on holiday and rented a cottage from Miss Wadland (in Roborough) for the summer. When Miss Wadland died, many of her possessions were offered in a house clearance sale. We were on holiday nearby at the time, and I bought a black ebony rod ruler which I remember being used to wrap knuckles or draw lines at the foot of the day's work. The ruler is lying on my desk now as I write this letter."

∞∞∞∞

Jean Folland (Maynard), 1947-1953

"Miss Wadland used to sit very upright in her chair at the head of the classroom table, and we were expected to do the same. If a child started to slacken in their chair, then they were in for trouble. Our lunch lasted approximately twenty minutes, then the class would go out to play, but Miss Wadland would usually organise the games. During art lessons Miss Wadland would sometimes get us to draw various things which we could see from the classroom window, including a war memorial. Mid-morning break (11.00 am), we would each have a bottle of milk then we would go outside and line up to do gym. If a child needed extra tuition, (perhaps leading up to their eleven plus exam), Miss Wadland would have them in on a Saturday morning. Our parents were given a written report at the end of each year."

∞∞∞∞

Rona Spencer (Budgett), 1949-1952

"I remember learning thoroughly by rote and repetition – was well ahead in Maths, English language (parsing) and French (written not spoken), when I went to boarding school at the age of eleven. I once recited a poem for a school inspector. Playing games in the garden with a mulberry tree in the centre. The hand bell to bring us into class. The boys flicking wet blotting paper onto the ceiling. Staying the night in a feather bed before sitting the eleven plus exam because we were snow bound."

∞∞∞∞

Jill Buckingham (Fishleigh), 1949-1954

"Miss Wadland used to come out into the garden while we were having our break. She would sit on a little stool under the mulberry tree and read us stories, mainly of Brer Rabbit."

∞∞∞∞

John Puddicombe, 1951-1953

"I remember Miss Wadland weeping when telling us of the death of King George VI. Later, I think I remember her reading passages to us from the newspaper about Captain Coulsen on the 'Flying Enterprise'."

∞∞∞∞

Anne Poore (Guy), 1952-1955

"I was a boarder at Miss Wadland's, and after school hours, we would go off for a walk, usually down West Lane or Stafford Road. We used to have night prayers just before we went to bed. I also remember going to St Edmond's Church to evensong, which was midweek. This happened from time to time as Miss Wadland was the organist. Miss Wadland loved music, and she often played the piano."

∞∞∞∞

Geraldine Stanley (Evans), 1950-1953

"I have to say that my years at Miss Wadland's school were not happy ones. I think that one would now say that there was a personality clash... I do remember much of that time quite clearly. There was a wonderful mulberry tree in the garden, around which we used to dance every day at break time. Each Christmas time we made cards from excellent quality card – we had to draw (free hand) either a lantern or holly which we then painted with watercolours. I was constantly in trouble for not getting it just right. I also remember

clearly the very tattered but colourful ABC book from which we were taught the alphabet. We learnt basic sums with the aid of beautiful polished shells (I think they were conch shells). I can still remember the room in which we were taught with an enormous table down the centre, around which we all sat. I think I was sent to stand in every corner of the room during my short time there!"

∞∞∞∞

Alida Pollard (Pickard), 1952-1958

"The only general impression that remains is that we were always aware that we were there to learn. She never made it seem a bore, and gave everyone a sense of their own worth. (A pity there aren't more like her today.) We were also made to stand on a box and speak correctly – no Devonian accent for Miss Wadland! She always encouraged interest in all things. On a school outing we went to see the Queen Mother pass through Eggesford Station."

∞∞∞∞

Richard Mendham, 1952-1958

"Of my memorable moments I remember dancing around the mulberry tree chanting particular songs; winter afternoons working in lamplight listening to wonderful stories of Adam and Eve, King Alfred etc; being allowed the privilege of tending the lamps; the smell of baked potatoes; Miss Wadland's sandals; demanding that I wore two vests when I took my eleven plus exam, ("you can't study if you're cold!"); being too big and vigorous for a lady of her age to contain. Nevertheless she taught me all I know, aesthetically speaking. Of her favourite sayings I remember "Empty barrels make most noise", "Do as you would be done by", "Richard, I'll tell your father!" and "The utmost for the highest."

Richard Mendham is now headmaster of his own school here in Devon.

∞∞∞∞

83

David West, 1952-1957

*"What a flood of memories you brought back! Some things
are clear in my mind as if they happened yesterday, others
are like elusive shadows that you can't quite get hold of and
keep slipping away. My earliest memory is of sitting on Miss
Wadland's knee learning the alphabet from a large picture
book, typical of the post-war period. I must have been four
and a half. We learned to write using soft pencils that
would rub out easily on specially drawn lines, and we
would practice until we got it right! The most important
things were pot hooks, loops, and to get all the uprights at
the same angle, not leaning backwards. French was very
difficult. Sometimes we would stand before the blackboard
in a small group trying her patience to the limit. One day I
was distracted and when my turn came to add the next part
of the verb I had lost all concentration. Miss Wadland was
so furious she picked up the map pointer, put me over her
knee, and hit me with it. Fortunately for me the pointer was
a flimsy piece of dowel or similar, and it broke, one piece flying up and hitting the ceiling. I seem to remember that
everyone laughed, including Miss Wadland, except me!*

*When lunch break came, two of the girls would lay the
table (feminists and sexism being unheard of then). A cloth
would be put over the grey baize, and each pupil would have
two plates, always one in front of the other, never side by
side. A small table at the end furthest from the window
would be set for Miss Wadland and her boarder(s) who
always had a cooked lunch. Each day pupil brought his
own lunch. After lunch we were allowed to play in the garden. There was a large ivy-covered tree in the left hand corner, and one day several of us climbed and "hid" in this tree.
Once again we must have tried Miss Wadland's patience no
end, as we wouldn't go in when the bell was rung. – A small
hand bell was rung at the end of the lunch hour, sometimes
by favoured pupils. We stayed up the tree, very daringly, for
about ten or fifteen minutes while Miss Wadland searched
for us, found us and ordered us to come down. Those less
daring than the rest gave in fairly quickly, while one or two
hung on for an extra few minutes to demonstrate their disre-
gard for authority! During the time I was there one pupil,*

Richard Mendham, was a particular trial to Miss Wadland. His behaviour swung from absolutely outrageous to being almost angelic. I'm sure that he's able to look back, and now being who he is, he understands he created problems.

On Fridays we used to finish school at midday, and often we children would pretend to hear a car hooter in order to go out and play at the bottom of the lane and on the opposite bank, on which grew a horse chestnut. One of Miss Wadland's jokes was to say that if we went out of the class-room door and turned right to face a cupboard door, that cupboard led to China. It was a long time before I dared open the door for fear of being led away by yellow skinned mandarins with long pigtails and black droopy moustaches. One day, having been sent out for behaving badly, I chanced a peep. Imagine my relief at seeing a cupboard full of china! Another day when I was sent out, I went out to the yard. A local boy, whose name I can't remember, (but I believe he used to live with his parents in South Africa and his first name was Peter) used to cycle to school, and I decided to ride his bicycle. Of course Miss Wadland came to look for me and caught me. I remember her difficulty in trying to keep a straight face! She must have had such a sense of humour. If only I'd appreciated it then.

I think I could summon up many more stories, but this seems to be turning into my own biography! Suffice to say that I remember your cousin as being held in great esteem by all the parents and later on, by many of the pupils. She gave a great deal to so many young people, not only through grounding in basic education, but something more which I can't put a name to."

∞∞∞∞

Maureen Martin (Deakin), 1954-1957

"If we misbehaved we were usually sent into Miss Wadland's study for about half an hour. I can remember several occasions when I was sent there. Miss Wadland just had to say my name in a certain tone, and I knew just from her look that I would end up in her study. On one occasion when I was in the study, I went to her desk where there was a leather-bound blotting pad. I licked my fingers and rubbed them over the blotting paper, making rolls and ending up with heaps of it on the floor. When Miss Wadland came in after my half hour punishment and saw what I had been doing, I ended up spending the rest of the morning in the study until lunchtime. Actually, I used to enjoy it in there as Miss Wadland had a lot of family portraits on the walls which I spent many a time looking at. Miss Wadland used to like the girls to do skipping, and when we out in the garden, she would tie one end of the rope to an old pear tree and get one of us to start jumping, then she would get the others to join in, ending up with about four or five of us. Miss Wadland always met her pupils at the door each morning when we arrived for school, and she would also see us off at the end of the day."

∞∞∞∞

Angela Earle (Green), 1954-1957

"Things that particularly stick in my mind were: the long school table with the youngest at one end and the eldest at the other; the piano; the maps of the world hanging above the blackboard; the older boys who were rather naughty sometimes; the verandah outside; the lovely back garden with the mulberry tree where we used to play; the outbuildings; my bedroom and oil lamp; the delicious high teas – especially the rock cakes and seed cakes; the nature walks after school down the "back lane" to the stream at the bottom; making Christmas cards and papier mache bowls in front of the fire in winter time.

I am so sorry I can only remember such a little. Miss Wadland must have been wonderful to us, as well as an excellent teacher. I am sorry I was too young to appreciate it at the time. I left early because of the behaviour of the boys! (my brother was one of them I'm afraid), but at my next state school, I was far too advanced education wise, to be put in a class of my appropriate age. Looking back Miss Wadland was a kind and brilliant teacher."

∞∞∞∞

86

Martin Grigg, 1952-1958

"Miss Wadland called her 'cooker' Frances, and each day before lunch she would say "I wonder what Frances has prepared for me today." A 'modulator' hung on one wall, and every morning we had to sing the notes from 'Doh to Doh' to get in tune for the hymn. We were never allowed in the front garden. On special occasions we played a game called French v English in the back garden. Miss Wadland also used to say "Little boys should be seen but not heard." When naughty we had to lie on a mat in a bedroom. She used to pull hair as a punishment, and one boy called Henry Chapman was nearly bald by the time he left school!

∞∞∞∞

Louise Noble (Budgett), 1954-1959

"How glad I am that you are writing Miss Wadland's biography. She was one of the earliest and certainly one of the most lasting influences on my life. I think of her frequently with affection and thankfulness. My memories are inevitably not chronological or organised but I hope you can make some sense and use of these jottings.

One of her favourite scripture passages was Philippians 4 v.8, often used to admonish us:

> Finally brothers, whatever is true,
> whatever is noble, whatever is right,
> whatever is pure, whatever is lovely,
> whatever is admirable – if anything is
> excellent or praiseworthy – think
> about such things.

> Philippians 4 v.8

No electricity at Sages when I first went; we had several "Tilly" lamps on the long table, which almost filled the room, and on winter evenings these produced a warm light and a sort of hum, not to mention a sporadic atmosphere. Even after electricity, I still had a little night light in my room. Electricity was marvellous, I used to read in bed, anything and everything. Usually I heard her footsteps as she came up, but if I didn't, and she spotted the light, the usual scenario was,

"Can't you sleep dear?"

"No Miss Wadland."

"Would you like a hot drink?"

"Yes please Miss Wadland."

I would be brought hot lemon or Bovril, which I sipped by the teaspoonful to finish the chapter!

In the mornings, after the other children arrived, I'd always be asked "what sort of mood is she in?" Sometimes I'd do a bit of dusting or tidying up before school, but I never went into the kitchen.

Pencil sharpeners were an anathema to her; we used to use a big knife over a sheet of newspaper.

At break time, in good weather, we went out into the back yard, sometimes into the garden where we had to run round by the path – I still have the scar on my knee where I tripped (or was tripped!), and she sat by me in the back entrance bathing it to get out the gravel. Sometimes we did skipping under the big mulberry tree; she and a favoured pupil turned the big rope. As a boarder I spent hours with a book up the ivy smothered trees in a "den". She never objected to honest dirt from climbing etc. She would not tolerate foul language. I know one unfortunate boy had to eat soap once.

French: When I went to boarding school at ten and a half, I soon realised my grammar was good but my accent got laughed at, so I had to forget Waddy's pronunciation. "Août" sticks in my mind as an embarrassing word. We used "le livre rouge", and sometimes read about Madame Souris. However even as O-Level approached I often found that new work like subjunctives seemed strangely familiar, so I think she taught us quite a lot.

Alphabet: We learned using rhymes in a book which began "A is for anchor, used at sea. You'll find some more upon the quay." She didn't approve of the one for 'C', so we said "C is for cat, on the cover". I'd had this book at home, so already knew the rhymes (and still remember quite a few!), so I was not popular with the other children.

Writing: We learned by joining dots, starting with lines

upwards and downwards: | | | |, then pot hooks: ᘘ ᴨ etc.
Pages of copying and flowery capitals, eg ℰ ℋℰ ℰ . I was
made to change at secondary school, as I was told it was too
ornate and illegible, but I still use ℐ etc for Russian!

Maths: We started with adding dots, then numbers. I
remember huge addition sums on the board, and she would
make us add up aloud, dodging round the whole school,
except the "tinies", and it had to be accurate, and fast!

Spelling: We had plenty of lists to learn, with rules. I
before E, except after C, if it rhymes with T.

History: She was particularly fond of early English history, especially King Alfred, as she used to live near where he
burned those cakes. I remember chanting dates but can't fit
the sequence of the kings to the numbers. The history text
book was yellow, and already collapsing.

Geography: We used a book with a page of text on one
side, and a picture to colour on the other, eg Pygmies,
Tundra etc. I remember my stepsister making a relief map of
South America in clay which was baked and painted.

Art: No free/self expression! We had books of squared
paper with designs, pictures from simple eg: ✗ ⊞ up to
highly complicated (I remember a farmer on a tractor) which
we had to copy exactly by joining the dots, and filling in the
colour blocks exactly to her example. At Christmas we painted cards using high quality stiff paper, As a boarder I
helped fold and cut it. Designs were also obligatory – bunches of balloons, by drawing round overlapping pennies,
stylised Christmas trees with candles, holly and berries.

Craft: Boys and girls did the same; raffia mats, or table
napkin rings, knitting dishcloths or garter stitch coat hanger
covers, crochet and bead work for milk jug covers, cone pen
trays using the base of date boxes. I know Waddy was
quite handy at wood-work herself, and I think quite proud of
it, in a way.

Singing: Hymns and well known songs, eg "Early one
morning", "Do ye ken John Peel?" "Polly Wolly Doodle." At
my request she taught me piano in the evenings. I went to
school in Sept '59, and passed Grades I & II in March '60, so
she took me quite far. I remember enjoying duets with her.

Reading: I remember we used a book with continued
'stories' to reinforce the learning of certain sounds. "'This'

and 'that' were two wretched kittens", and we endured this, not only reading it ourselves, but listening to others struggling.

Pupil-teacher system: As we progressed up the school, and up towards the head of a long table, we were encouraged when we had finished our assignment, to go down to one of the 'tinies' for whom we were responsible, look at what they were doing, listen to reading, guide their hands with pot hooks etc. I was with a tot called Ailsa. As a boarder, for some time the only one. I used to sit opposite Waddy in the evenings. She marked the seniors' books, I did some of the little ones'. I knew, from the age of about eight that I wanted to be a teacher, as indeed I was, though when the time came I chose languages at secondary, not infant work though I was torn between the two. "Waddy" was a role model for me. Possibly the most useful thing she taught any of us was the ability to concentrate on our own work while others in the school were doing different things. there were about eighteen of us, so only three or four in each work group. her organisation was obviously exceptional.

One of her favourite stories deriding herself was that one day, during the school hours, someone knocked at the door. She set the school to work, took the visitor into the 'best' room alongside, where she plied the young man with coffee and biscuits trying to think which of her former pupils he could possibly be. Only eventually did she realise he was an H.M.I!

On one occasion, someone broke a flower-pot in the garden. We had to sit round the table in silence until the guilty party owned up, which I think took most of the afternoon. it wasn't me but I felt and looked so embarrassed for whoever it was, though I didn't know who, and lots of people thought I'd done it.

There was a stuffed owl in a glass case at the head of the stairs next to the loo. I believe the owl came from her childhood home and was known as Billy.

Meals: I suspect we must have had stews quite a lot, or at any rate meals which looked after themselves. She and the boarders ate at midday. I still remember egg sandwiches (brown bread, chopped hard boiled egg) in summer evenings for picnics, and I still have a fondness for Sago (not shared by my family: "frog spawn"!) Waddy's was creamy, delicious, and strongly flavoured with lemon by infusing the peel.

When I was a boarder Waddy would often brush my hair for me at bedtime, which I loved. She would tell me how she used to do it as a girl for her mother.

Her favourite sayings were "I'm as old as my little finger, and a little older than my teeth", if age was debated; "I'll go and see what Florence has for us today", referring to lunch for herself and the boarders – the cook was Florence.

School motto: "The utmost for the highest."

Occasionally we'd go over to the church together, where she was organist for years. She never said so but I now feel sure she must have prayed a lot for all of us, her pupils. She certainly seems to me to have been a very godly influence."

ooooooo

Julie Soper (Grigg), 1954-1961

"Sages and Miss Wadland will always remain in my memory for many reasons. I thought Miss Wadland's was the usual run-of-the-mill primary school, but as I got older and spoke to children from state schools, I realised Sages was definitely a one-off! I will try to recall for you some of my memories, although they have, of course, become clouded with time.

I can vividly remember the school room – a large room, French windows at one end, and the huge school table in the middle housing two/three 'Tilly' lamps around which we all sat, the young ones at one end going up to the oldest pupils at the French window end. On one side of the room was a big map of the world (she also possessed an old and well-used globe), a wall hanging used for teaching singing – it had the Doh Ra Me Fa etc. on it. – I'm sure Miss Wadland used to call it the 'modulator.' I can remember each morning we used to line up in two rows on the sideboard side of the room and sing a hymn and say prayers accompanied by Miss Wadland on the piano or occasionally one of the pupils who could play the piano.

At lunch time we all used to bring a packed lunch and

eat it around the big table. This was accompanied by Miss Wadland firing questions at us around the table such as countries, capitals and the rivers they stand on, English counties and their capitals, and multiplication tables. I can still recite virtually every capital of every country and the river they stand on! Miss Wadland would also read a book to us after lunch – I can remember particularly, "The Water Babies", "Romulus and Remus", and "The Wind in the Willows". If the weather was particularly good, we would go into the garden and do country dancing – The Cumberland Square Eight springs to mind – and invariably we would end up trying not to laugh when Miss Wadland caught her hairnet on the mulberry tree in the garden. The number of times that hairnet had to be salvaged!

I can remember Miss Wadland vividly – the grey hair pulled back into a bun at the back of her head and all held in place by the ever-present hairnet! She had a preference for navy blue which she always wore in some form or another. In fact I seem to remember her having the name 'the blue dragon'!

I really can't say with all honesty that I 'enjoyed' my schooldays. I never hated it and there was never a time that I had to be 'dragged' to school. I can remember many a time wondering why we did this or learnt that. I know now, because Miss Wadland's basic educational grounding was the best. It stood us in great stead for our further education and still draw on the information she imparted to us. I wish my own children could have had the advantage of the basic groundwork education that I had. She was an amazing woman – there were few like her, even all those years ago, and certainly none to match her teaching skills nowadays.

My mother said that when the fees had to go up from eight guineas to ten guineas, Miss Wadland apologised profusely for having to do it because of the price of books, etc and my mother said she can remember it well because in their opinion it was still very reasonable fees to charge even with the rise!"

∞∞∞∞

Pricilla West, 1954-1959

"Memorable moments: Just that it was a delight in retrospect and living the life at the time! I once cheated in a Friday morning test and with no word, Miss Wadland sent me to the 'back room' where I sat for some time. When she came she sat me on her lap with no word – I cried – she hugged me – and I never did it again!"

∞∞∞∞

Catherine Wright (Ellis), 1956-1957

"Items that particularly stick in the mind: The contrast with the village school (Winkleigh) where I had previously been, eg the insistence on shading when painting flowers, Greek Myths, French, education seen as serious and decorous."

∞∞∞∞

Maralyn Fraser (Stacey), 1958-1961

"Items that particularly stick in the mind: It was terrifying – she was so strict. We were put in the corner corridor or sent upstairs. I fell asleep on the bed once which made it worse. We were always in tears. I remember the alphabet chart, it had some weird words like 'A is for anchor'. The history dates filled a board – we had to remember them, 1066 was the only one I knew. I remember the best room next door where eleven plus tests were done, and we had tests on Fridays. There was a lovely old mulberry tree in the garden – I've probably never seen another. We used to have PT outside. I'm sure there was a cobbled area and we would march around the garden for deportment."

∞∞∞∞

93

Joyce Gillard (Williams), 1955-1957

"In the years immediately after World War II my family lived in Beaford, about two miles or so from Dolton, and my parents, being dissatisfied with the village school, enrolled my elder brother and I in Miss Wadland's school at Sages in Dolton. We travelled there daily in the village taxi owned and run by an elderly man called Mr White. There were actually five of us who made the journey, Roger and I, Bridget Moger, Nicholas and Anita Patterson. The Patterson children lived in Kenya but in view of the Mau Mau terrorist attacks, they were sent home to the safety of the Devon countryside. For the first year I was a day pupil. I clearly recall my first day, I was given a copybook and the first few lines were intended to give Miss Wadland an idea of how good (or bad) my penmanship was. Scrutinising my shaky delivery which I could see was not good, she decided that I should begin the process from square one , and I was taught strokes \\\\ , and pothooks \\.\)\ – her initiation into the world of good handwriting. Miss Wadland was capable of getting the most, in terms of performance, from all the students in her care. She had infinite patience and was very thorough. I never remember her losing her temper or raising her voice but neither do I remember disobeying a command! Looking back, I realise her days were so full that she must have been extremely well organised. To oversee the study programme for children working at so many levels, to teach piano, to coach students for entrance exams, to cook all the meals well, despite rationing, to take a daily walk during which we discussed the flora and fauna, the cloud formations etc, to do her turn at the altar flowers, play the organ for all the Church services, to help with the various bazaars; her life could not have been fuller. At the time that I was at school, we had no electricity in either house or church. We studied and worked by lamps which I know (now) as Coleman lanterns. Upon arriving at school in the mornings we had a hymn and a prayer and this was followed by singing a couple of times a week, it was Miss Wadland's goal to get everyone singing, however reluctant they might have been. I recall that Nicholas West was particularly reluctant. We learned to pitch notes, to sing scales, I can't remember many

of the songs but I do still know 'Early One Morning' and 'Pansy Faces'. Another daily ritual which proved invaluable in the years to come was the mental arithmetic exercises we practiced, in which columns of numbers were written on the blackboard and we raced to fill in the totals, (Richard Hopper's special forté).

When we took our places at the table, lessons began in earnest. We sat at a large rectangular table; Miss Wadland's seat at the foot was surrounded by the youngest children and as you got older you moved further away from this homebase, until by the time you were eleven, you were at the other end of the table. Before the start of my second year my family moved down into Cornwall, and it was somehow agreed that I would continue as one of Miss Wadland's pupils, but would now live with her for the duration of the school year. It was the start of three years of well-ordered and secure childhood. On Sundays Miss Wadland would go to Holy Communion at 8.00 am, and than after breakfast we would go to eleven o'clock matins service. We also attended evensong. This was not so much because of an excess of religious zeal as because Miss Wadland was the Anglican Church organist. In the absence of the Rev. Haslam, the services were conducted by Maj. Sir Ralph Furse, who was elderly and very deaf. This deafness caused some confusion where congregational responses were called for. There were either long pauses, or not enough pauses so we waited patiently for him to try to keep up. I remember Miss Wadland telling me about a trip to Switzerland. Apparently she was sitting with friends watching a firework display when a burning ember drifted down and burned a hole in her evening dress. This was, apparently, rather a serious mishap from an economic and logistical point of view. Sounds like an episode from "Little Women" don't you think? I think of Miss Wadland always with affection and gratitude. She instilled in me a love of music and books and also a lively curiosity about people and places. My life has been richer, in no small measure, because of her tutelage."

∞∞∞∞

Henry Chapman, 1955-1959

"Memorable moments: Yes, but not the kind you want to hear about. The time Dr West did 100mph on Beaford straight taking us home from school. How we used to pretend to Miss Wadland that our car had come early to collect us, and then we played in the village for half an hour.

Items that particularly stick in my mind: I can always remember playing British Bulldog in the garden under the mulberry tree. I can remember running around the garden for 'keep fit'. The smell of Miss Wadland's cooking for her boarders lunch – the huge table we all sat around and the French windows."

∞∞∞∞

Paul Longridge-Berry, 1956-1962

"Miss Wadland was a marvellous teacher but quite strict. She certainly gave me a good start, education wise, and took pride in getting her pupils through the eleven plus."

∞∞∞∞

Christine Lucas (Brickel), 1959-1961

"I remember your cousin as being a fairly tall stout lady with grey hair mostly tied back in folded plaits around her head, and wearing glasses. I don't have any fond memories of Miss Wadland. Frankly, I think she was an old tyrant. However, as a young child not knowing her very well, one could easily have that impression of her, but it was nothing more than because Miss Wadland was strict, and there is nothing wrong in that, for it gives a child good discipline. My brother has no fond memories of her, and didn't want to contribute towards this book."

∞∞∞∞

*Left: Sarah Wadland,
'the favourite Aunt'.*

*Right: Miss Alice Wadland,
c. 1930*

This photograph was taken on 6th July 1895, of the Wadland family outside the family home of Owlacombe, Roborough in North Devon. It depicts Mr and Mrs Richard Wadland on the day of their daughter's baptism (Eliza 'Margaret' Wadland). The children pictured on the back row from left to right are May Wadland, Winifred Wadland and Henry Lawrence Wadland. The two girls at the front are...

Mrs Eliza Wadland

Miss Sarah Wadland

Margaret Wadland, Alice's sister, pictured with the family pony

The annual summer tea-party at Aller Court c. 1907. Richard and Eliza Wadland and three of their daughters, together with a maid, are pictured on the right hand side.

Travelling bears in France c. 1905, something which Alice and her parents also witnessed during their continental travels.

Richard Wadland (centre) with workmen on the Aller estate.

*Aller Church,
where the Wadlands
worshipped for 13 yrs*

*Left: Miss Kathleen
Wadland, who was
often pictured holding
a book as if to remind
the viewer of her
scholarly talents*

*Right: Alice's pet
owl which she had
during her childhood.*

Snapshot of Aller Court House

Henry Lawrence Wadland, pictured
in uniform shortly before he was sent
to the Western front.

Lt. R. A. Faire and Lt. E. G.
Holyoak, who were close friends of
the Wadland girls, pictured here at
Army Camp.

Back row:, left to right: Lilian Chammings, Gwen Bellew, Vera Blackmore
Front row, left to right: Joyce Chammings, Marjorie Chammings, Nancy Holwill

This is the earliest group photo known to exist of Alice's pupils. The photo was
lent to the author by Mrs Mary Gent (daughter of Vera Blackmore), and is
reproduced with her kind permission

Alice Wadland in the garden of Sages, c. 1954. Note the upturned stool on which Alice used to sit when reading stories under the mulberry tree.

Group photo taken at Sages c. 1954.
Back row, left to right: Nicholas West, Jean Maynard, Bridget Moger, Jill Fishleigh
Front row, left to right: Colin West, ?, ?, Mary Maynard

Both of the photos on this page are reproduced with the kind permission of
Mrs Jill Buckingham, nee Fishleigh

The Matterhorn, Switzerland, which Alice and her more reluctant sister Kathleen climbed.

Mountain range in the region of Lauterbrunnen, a place explored by Alice and her sisters.

Snapshot of Alice in the garden of Sages

Snapshot of Mrs Eliza Wadland in the garden of Sages

A rare moment of relaxation. Alice is pictured on the right, her mother in the centre and her sister Winifred on the left.

*Portrait photograph of
Elsie Wadland*

*Portrait photograph of
Kathleen Wadland c. 1905*

Portrait photograph
of Alice Wadland

Sages, Dolton, c.1920. This photograph was taken by Mr William (Bill) Clements (who was himself a keen tennis player) depicting some of Dolton's tennis players.
Standing extreme left in the back row is Alfred Line. Alice Wadland is 3rd from left and next to her is Harold Selly, Charlie Fishleigh and Mr Bull. First left in the middle row is Dorothy Wills. Mr Clements was unable to identify the remainder of the ladies due to their faces being hidden by their hats.

This photograph was taken by Mrs Jean Lock, (nee Heal) and is re-produced with her kind permission. It was taken in 1953, during the coronation, and depicts Alice Wadland walking towards Dolton village square, with Shute House behind her. When Alice spotted Jean taking the photo she had no intention in pausing for a moment, but continued her walk in full stride.

SOUTHOVER,
DOLTON,
WINKLEIGH,
North Devon.

October 16th. 1971 -

Dear Mrs Lynch Blosse

You and Sylvia and all of you, have not been out of my thoughts since this morning when Margery shocked me with the almost unbelievable news about your dear David.

Added to your personal grief, and not knowing the procedure, I fear that you must be going through an extremely harrowing time, and I cannot imagine how you are coping. If we could _do_ anything helpful we should be only too thankful.

We are truly concerned about you and the children, and pray that you will be given the fortitude to be brave.

My sister joins me in sending love and heartfelt sympathy -

Alice Wadland -

Copy of a letter which Alice sent to Evangeline Lynch-Blosse, the mother of Sir David Lynch-Blosse, Bt., Alice's first boy pupil

Alice pictured standing by the apple tree in the garden of Southover c. 1970

Three views of the commemorative jug (see also overleaf) made by Harry Juniper of Bideford. Commissioned by the author, it celebrated the centenary of Alice's birth, and through its publicity it brought more people forward who attended her school. The jug stands at a height of ten inches.

Cmdr. George T.Moger (parent)

"Yes, my daughter Bridget Esme Moger went to her school in Dolton for, I think, about two years 1948-50, and then pined to board at St Catherine's School in Bude. We bought North Harepath Farm, Beaford, in March 1948, leaving in 1954 when Bridget went to Sherbourne School. Miss Wadland gave her a very good grounding, particularly in arithmetic, and she was a charming woman of the "old school", just what young children needed (and still do but no longer get it and hence many of today's troubles!). Of course, as you probably know, she was known as "Waddleduck" to us!"

∞∞∞∞

Mrs Josephine Wills (parent)

"At the time I met Alice Wadland, my husband was a Surrey Army officer with the Devonshire Regiment, and we were living in army quarters near Exeter with our two sons. The elder, Michael aged fourteen, was at boarding school, and David was aged four. We had at that time been around the world where education for English families serving overseas was poor, and in some cases non-existent. So, when my husband was posted overseas again, I decided to remain in England, where David starting school could have a good and uninterrupted period of education. As I had to leave my quarters at Topsham, I consulted Agents for furnished accommodation in Devon, and hopefully to find a school nearby. Before embarking on this venture, I decided to have a short holiday with my sister in Yorkshire. On the morning of our departure, a neighbour brought me some magazines, amongst which was the current 'Lady'. I hurriedly scanned through the adverts and found one for 'Long Lets' in Dolton. I replied to the address, giving the explanation that I would be in Yorkshire for two weeks, and also giving details of myself and of my son Michael at boarding school, and for some unknown reason I did not mention my son David. The Lord was surely guiding my pen, as I will explain later. I had a reply from Miss Wadland by return of post, asking me to visit her. I cut short my holiday and returned home when

I made an appointment to see this Miss Wadland, and view the cottage. On the journey to Dolton lots of thoughts went through my mind, whether I should have gone with my husband, as the countryside became more rural and seemingly so remote. On arrival at Dolton square, I was met by a very tall elegant lady dressed in black, with a hat, handbag and gloves, although she only lived a short distance away. I liked her on sight, but she said "You didn't mention in your letter that you had a small child." If I had she would not have replied to my letter, as her last tenants, a squadron leader's family had wrecked her home, and had used her furniture as trampolines. I assured her that this sort of behaviour would not be allowed in my house. She took us to her home and gave us lunch, and then to the cottage which I was to rent. She showed me through the cottage and where everything was, and then said, "I will leave you here and you must go into each room, and sit a short time in each, and then go and have a walk around the village, and by that time you will have made up your mind. If you want to live here then come and have tea with me when you return home."

There was a very large apple tree in the garden, and David found his way up there, and shouted down to me, "I want to stay here, I don't want to go back to Exeter." I explained that we had to go back, to pack up all our possessions, he insisted that we hire someone to do it, as he did not wish to go back. He convinced me that this was right for him as well as right for me. We returned to Miss Wadland's for tea, and during tea she told me that she ran a private school. I could not believe my good fortune. David started at her school, and although he only spent a few years with her, the good grounding and her unique teaching abilities, helped him when he went to Kings, Rochester, Kent and later to Sandhurst. He is now a Brigadier. So many children taught by Alice Wadland won scholarships to public schools, and are now fully equipped to serve the community in various professions. She had only one failure in all her years of teaching. When this biography is published. a copy should be sent to various schools. In my opinion there would be fewer children leaving school unable to read, if they used her methods.

Another little story about Alice Wadland, she was fiercely independent, never asked for help, or expected it. One day, when I arrived at her school with David, she was in a state of distress, hair not done, running a very high temperature. I told her to go back to bed at once, and I would take all her pupils to my house, and look after them for the day. I asked Dr West (whose children attended her school) to look after her. All went well, and in the afternoon I took the children for a walk round the village. I met a woman who inquired why I was looking after Alice Wadland's pupils. I replied that she was ill, and I had told her to go to bed. She said "I can't believe it, you had the nerve to tell Miss Wadland to go to bed, no one tells Miss Wadland what to do." I did not find her awesome, she was a very Christian woman, and worked endlessly for the Church, and humanity in general."

∞∞∞∞

Angela Pritchard (Stacey), 1962-1965

"Items that particularly stick in my mind: Deportment – having to march around the table with an encyclopedia on your head; Dancing around the mulberry tree (which the squirrels used to ruin!); The smell of Pears soap in the cloakroom; Oil lamp on the grey blanket covered table; the wooden shutters being closed in winter."

THE APPLE TREE
& APPLE PASTIES (1963 - 1972)

With the closing chapter at Sages, in the summer months of 1963, Alice and Kathleen started preparations for the move, (during the summer holidays) to Southover. Alice had bought Southover on the 30th of April 1928 when it was then known as 'Rose Cottage'. Alice paid a Mrs Anne Drummond £250.00 for the property, Anne Drummond was the wife of the late Dr Alexander Drummond, and when they acquired the property, the doctor had a large room built on the side of the cottage which was to house his library. When Alice moved in, the room was to be her new classroom. In the early years, she let the property as short holiday lets, then with her increasing workload at school, she decided to change over to long lets. The property during that time was also rented by people who sent their children to Alice's school. Southover is located in Aller road at the top of Stafford Hill, and on the corner into Chapel Street. It's a most charming thatched property with quaint rooms. In one corner of the front garden stands the lovely old bramley apple tree, of which former pupils will have fond memories. Alice was renowned throughout her school years in Dolton for her 'apple pasties'. When she was at Arscotts and Sages, she would always serve them hot, and topped with clotted cream. The boarders thought this to be a special treat, however, quietly, it caused much envy amongst the day pupils, who sat at the same table, with just packed lunches.

Whilst reminiscing, several former pupils mentioned the stuffed 'Barn Owl' which Alice had in a glass case. The children obviously had a great fascination for it. The owl had once been a pet of Alice's during her childhood, having received it as a casualty which Alice nursed back to full recovery. Sadly, the poor owl lost its life when it was flying through a doorway, a gust of wind slammed the door shut and caught the unfortunate bird.

∞∞∞

Angela Allin (Underhill), 1960 - 1966

"At the beginning of each day Miss Wadland would start with prayers, then at 11 am we had a bottle of milk, followed by exercises. Grace was always said before lunch. All pupils would take their own lunch. Each child was given two plates and a cup. The plates would be placed in front of us, then once our lunch boxes were opened, we would empty the contents onto one of the plates. We then took one item at a time and placed it on the immediate plate, thus ready for eating. It was quite a performance."

∞∞∞

Sally Heal (Down), 1960 - 1967

"One of Miss Wadland's favourite sayings was 'Tummy in, tail in, tongue still'."

∞∞∞

Simon Berry, 1963 - 1968

"Item that particularly sticks in the mind: Collecting spiders from the bathroom and having races across the table when Miss Wadland wasn't looking.

Another of her sayings: 'I never like my pupils to be late! Time wasted can never be made up'."

∞∞∞

Nicola Fleming (Frey), 1963 - 1968

"Another one of her sayings: 'The Devil finds work for idle hands'."

∞∞∞

Martyn Fowler, 1967 - 1968

"Placing our sandals in racks each morning. Writing with an old ink pen and pencils. Reading from a lectern. I have fond memories. She was very strict with much discipline."

∞∞∞

Charmaine Leatt, 1964 - 1968

"I remember that if you swore you literally had your mouth washed out with soap and water – it never happened to me, but I saw it happen to someone else!

We did morning maths and afternoon maths, in consequence of which, when I had to change schools in 1968 I was way ahead in that subject.

We had P.E and danced to good old tunes like "The Grand Old Duke of York."

The children at school had this way of getting any child that was out of line into line, by declaring 'war' on them. This was like Coventry, and included giving the victim the chipped plate at lunchtime. I was subject to this for half a day for being cheeky – it didn't last long because I cried when I got the chipped plate."

∞∞∞

Penny McLoughlin (Walker), 1962 - 1963

"Memorable moments: Enjoyed the drawing lessons, I was taught to shade balloons, and also to draw a coat hanging up on a peg behind the door. A love of art has remained. She was very patient and made me "see" the theory, so that I could do it."

Andrew Pickard, 1965 - 1968

"Memorable moments: A pupils losing a glass-eye which we all tried to find. Somebody having their mouth washed out with soap and water for swearing. Every Thursday my mother used to be invited in to have tea with Miss Wadland and her sister, and they always played cards called 'Old Maid'."

∞∞∞∞

Helen Watts (May), 1965 - 1968

"I remember Miss Wadland as being a kindly old lady, who taught each of us separately. She painstakingly taught us to write properly, and to do our sums, going around the table to each. Sometimes she would have small groups of the same age and stage on the other side of the room, and each would have to read in turn."

∞∞∞∞

ENGLISH v DEVONIAN

A local person who knew Alice well was Mrs Emmie Cockram, and she can recall Alice once saying jokingly "When my pupils come to school I get them speaking in moderate English, but at the end of the day, they go away speaking two languages, ie English and Devonian!"

The above anecdote related to how some of the children who originated from other parts of the country were influenced by some of the local fraternity in Alice's school, who had rather strong Devonian accents. Alice was well-known, that as she was running a private school, then there was no place for any accents. However, as we all know, children are impressionable, and some of the 'outsiders' fell into the vernacular at times, much to Alice's aggravation. From certain accounts it appears that some of the boys were trying to annoy Alice. In actual fact, I remember Helen Turrall once saying that her husband (Col. Hugh Turrall) when serving out in North Africa, during World War

103

II (for a period of five years without leave) was on one occasion out in the middle of some desert walking over some sand dunes wishing he was back in North Devon amongst the green hills, and as he was approaching the top of one dune, he heard a group of men speaking broad Devonian, and he said it was like music to his ears. Obviously it had the opposite effect on Alice's ears, although she evidently saw the lighter side of it, after all, she was a Devonian herself.

∞∞∞∞

A TRADITIONALIST, ROYALIST AND A TEAR

This may come as a surprise, and perhaps even a disappointment, to some women reading this, but Alice was not distinct in the sense of being a radical feminist. However I don't think that this is surprising, from what has already been said in this book. Alice was very much a traditionalist, and this seemed to be the legacy from her conventional Victorian background. A number of people have said that Alice's views were quite clear, that whether at home or at work, women should keep to their own place. Others have said "Miss Wadland would never have approved of feminism or womens' lib." I can only say, who really knows? We have to remember that the major populace of women were only just beginning to find their own footing in society during the 1900s, with the added determination of the campaigning by the suffragettes who transformed many of the conventional ideologies of the establishment. Perhaps had Alice been living today, in this very fast changing world, she may have held very different views on women, and their place in society.

Of all the girls, Alice's sister Winifred was the feminist and the most radical, and certainly not the ordinary 'run of the mill' type. It's obvious that Alice disliked some of Winifred's views and actions, but perhaps quietly she admired, yet at the same time envied, her sister. We also have to bear in mind that living in a small community like Dolton, had Alice been too radical, then that may have offended the conventional. Another item of anecdotal interest was the fact that Alice and Winifred shared the same birth date, i.e. 16th September. So, no doubt there must have been some affinity between them. Winifred outwardly was always a very compassionate individual, and although we know that Alice was the same underneath, she palpably suppressed her emotions.

Being very much a traditionalist, Alice's views with regard to the monarchy were unquestionable; a staunch royalist, who believed that the monarchy was the foundation stone of what held our society together. She was one of the dying few who believed in the divine appointment of our sovereigns. Former pupils remember well the morning after the death of King George VI in 1952, Alice sombrely walked into the classroom, then with a choked voice and tears in her eyes, made the sad announcement.

A M W

POEMS

SOUTHOVER SCHOOL 1963 - 1968

The following pages contain a wonderful selection
of poetry written by Alice's pupils.

A M W

A ROBIN

I saw
A robin on a tree
It was
An apple tree
He pecked
An apple rosy red
Just the colour
Of it's breast
He pecked
And then he flew
Away
Little robin
Come again
Another day
Come and build a nest

Southover School
Ages 6 yrs - 10yrs.

109

END OF TERM

What a hustle!
What a bustle!
End of term is here.

What a noise
Make the boys
Putting their books away
Take your pencils
Take your comb
You'll need them every day.

Take down the cord
Of the yellow quoit board
And pack school things away.

Rachel Davies 9 yrs.

NIPPER

I have a dog called Nipper
I like him very much
He sometimes gets the slipper
But it's just a little touch

He often pulls a cart of wood
And that is very good
And after working all the day
He sleeps well on a bed of hay

Angela Jane Stacey
8yrs 4months

SIR WINSTON CHURCHILL

Carriages abound
People all around
He was a great man
And I think Dad can
Remember the words he said.

His funeral was in state
The procession it was great
But it's too late
To meet him
The Great Sir Winston Churchill.

He was a commoner
Who had the funeral of a king
Many people saw it
It was a great thing.

People came from far away
From Africa and Gaul
They all met to say goodbye
Under the dome of St Paul.

Rachel Davies. 9yrs.

The wind is blowing from the north
It's blowing with all it's might
Today it's September the fourth
It may be worse in the night.

The wind is blowing from the west
It's a nice day for May
It's early morning so the people are at rest
This is the month of my birthday.

The wind is blowing from the south
This is the month of June
It must be nice at the river mouth
Tonight, it's just new moon.

The wind is blowing from the east
Now it's very cold
It's still warm inside at least
Look at the sun, a ball of gold.

Charmaine Leatt. 7yrs. 1/3/68

SPRING

Spring, Spring, Spring
The lambs begin to play
The birds begin to sing
Every minute of the day.

The cuckoo comes in Spring
And steals another's nest
Children hear the cuckoo sing
In Spring, Spring, Spring

Bright new green leaves
Sprout from the trees
The children swim
In the deep blue seas.

The sun shines bright
The days are long
It's all a pretty sight
In Spring Spring Spring.

Angela Underhill. 11 yrs.

MY TRAIN SET

In my train set I have
Engine, coach and truck.
Many rails on which they run
But sometimes they get stuck!

Some trucks have eight wheels
Some have four instead
All the rest are coaches
Painted blue and green and red.

Ian Frey. 10yrs.

SPRING

Goodbye to winter
Springtime is here
The air's getting warmer
For summer is near.

Birds cheeping merrily
Up in the trees
Blossoming flowers
Make work for the bees.

Days are getting longer
More time for my play
There's so many things
To do in a day.

Primroses, daisies,
Daffodils too
Yellow ones, white ones
Pink and blue.

Ewes are listening
Lest they should fear
A fox or a badger
Coming near

Easter chicks crack
Their hard egg-shell
While mother hen watches
To make sure that all's well.

Rachel Davies. 11 yrs.

THE LONE WOLF

A wolf escaped from the zoo
Whatever can we do?
But the wolf, he found
Being out of bound
Was not much fun.
He'd rather be in his bed
Than be full of lead
Alas! He was shot
But it meant a lot
To the owners of the sheep
Their lambs in safety to keep.

Rachel Davies. 9 yrs.

THE MIRACLE

I've been given sixpence to spend
And I'm going to the shop
Mummy said she would lend
Me a mac as mine is torn.

But, oh dear, I've dropped it
And I can't find it again
For I've dropped it in a pit
Alas! What shall I do.

But I found it again one day
In a huge bundle of hay
And for sweets it will pay
A miracle was that not?

Gay Leatt 10 yrs.

FROM MY WINDOW

From my window I can see
Little birds as free as free
The fields are brown and green and red
Yellow ones too I can view from my bed.

A few months ago the grass was grown
Now every field has been cut and mown.
And from my window I have heard a sound
The sound of the turner going around.

In the field there is a well
Quite hard to distinguish but I can tell
As by it lies a rotten log
On which I've played with my little dog

Rachel Davies. 9yrs.

PAIGNTON ZOO

I went to Paignton Zoo
On Thursday
And there I saw
A lot of bears and monkeys too
With their babies.
And next I saw a new
Penguin pond.
I heard a lion roar
And then I saw
A rather funny looking animal,
It ran at me
I ran away.
And as I was looking
At another animal
I fell and hurt my knee
And then I saw
A lot of donkeys
And longed to hear them bray
There were cows and sheep beyond
And ducks swam on a pond
It was a happy day
And this all quite true
Of what I saw at Paignton Zoo.

Angela Underhill. 10yrs.

A THUNDER STORM

Crack! Another branch has fallen
Pounded by the wind and rain.
Rumble! Another clap of thunder
Shaking every window pane.

Now the sky is lighted
By the lightening flashing fast
While down the gutter running, rolling
The gathered water rushed past.

People carrying black umbrellas
Rushing up and down the roads
Cars and buses, blowing hooters at
Lorries and vans with heavy loads.

Now the rain is getting slower
It will soon be at a stop
For the wind is surely dropping
And the rain will help the crop.

Rachel Davies 11yrs.

CAMPING

I strolled along to a little wood
My knapsack filled with lots of food
I pitched my tent beside a stream
Because I thought it nice and clean.

I heard a splashing in the stream
Alas! not a thing or person to be seen
Feeling weary and very tired
I went to bed and had a dream.

I hastened to get some water hot
And soon the tea was in the pot
I had my breakfast then and there
What a pity there was none to share!

I woke next morning while yet it was dark
I'm sure I heard a big dog bark
I ran to see but nothing was there
I must have been dreaming twas but a scare.

Simon Berry 9 yrs.

THE SEASONS

Spring is past
It goes very fast
It is like a clock
With a fast tick-tock.

The Summer is warm
The sun rises ... dawn
We shall go out to the sea
Before it is time for tea.

In Autumn back comes the wind
It whistles noisily in the key-hole
Ladies hats are securely pinned
The leaves whirl about on the knoll.

Winter is coming
Soon it will be snowing
The wind is still blowing
And so ends my poem.

Charmaine Leatt Aged 7.

THE WIND

The wind is blowing from the north
How cold it seems today!
It freezes all the winter troughs
And brings the snow to stay.

The wind is blowing from the west
Full of clouds and rain
The parched fields now full of zest
Are green and fresh again.

The wind is blowing from the south
in summer it's soft and warm
A lovely time for holidays
With cream teas on the lawn.

The wind is blowing from the east
I don't mind the cold
A woolly hat and an extra coat
Just as I am told.

Simon Berry 10 yrs. March 1st 1968.

THE MIRACLE

Jesus born on Christmas Day
Born in a stable full of hay
At a wedding he did something fine
Turned the water into wine

This miracle was his first
And the scribes him cursed
But he did it many times again
To heal the blind and heal the lame

On Good Friday in his Sepulchre he lay
To rise again on Easter Day
He conquered death and the grave
We his children for to save.

Rachel Davies. 10 yrs.

SUNSHINE

The sunshine shines on my pony's back
As I gallop across the moor
The sunshine shines in the babbling stream
And upon the bathroom floor.

The dew on the flowers shine
Like diamonds and gems they gleam
Like a beautiful ray of sunshine
A pure, pure golden beam.

The sunshine shines on the new lounge table
The sunshine shines on the floor
And the sunshine shines through every window
And shines for evermore.

Rachel Davies 10yrs.

FROM MY BEDROOM WINDOW

From my bedroom window
I see the rose red
I see them red
All flowering in their bed.
Also I can see, grass and a leafy tree.
The busy bee.
The colour of the flowers, blue and pink
And red, and all the green
Trees swaying to and fro.
For it's summer once again
The sheep and lambs are being sheared
For the weather's hot
From my bedroom window
Now I see a lot.

Simon Berry 7 yrs.

SUNSHINE

The Sunshine brings us pretty flowers
And warms us as we play
It brings us many happy hours
On a warm and sunny day.

If we had no sunshine
No crops would ever grow
And we would all be shivering
As cold and white as snow.

When I get up on winter days
It's still quite dark outside
But soon the sun lights up the sky
And all the stars do hide.

Nicola Frey 7 yrs.

BROKEN ARM ENDS OVER 50 YEARS OF TEACHING

MORE than half a century of teaching has been ended—by a broken arm. The injury has caused Miss Alice Wadland, who has been running a private school at her home at Southover, Dolton, for many years to retire, and the school has been wound up.

Miss Wadland is over 80, and her long years of service to the community is to be recognised next month by a presentation by parents of children she has taught.

A special tea party is planned at Heanton Satchville on May 1, after which she will be presented with a silver salver and a cheque for £70 by Lady Clinton.

Debt of gratitude

Mr. Bernard Leatt, Clerk to Torrington Rural Council, who, as a parent, helped organise an appeal, said: "The district owes Miss Wadland a great debt of gratitude.

"She has been teaching children, about 10-15 at a time, at her house and she has done a grand job.

"We feel we could not let the opportunity of her retirement go by without some expression being made of our appreciation."

Some of the children who have passed through Miss Wadland's hands recently are grandchildren of her first pupils.

TOO HOUSE-PROUD TO BE HAPPY

DID you read the letter to a woman's magazine recently quoting a neighbour's description of their home as being "clean enough to be healthy and dirty enough to be happy"?

It made one recall an old lady friend who would come beaming to see me, for it was somewhere (she said) where she could always feel comfortable.

She lived with a very house-proud sister, the kind to shake the doormat after anyone had come through the front door, always brushing up specks of dust and crumbs, and generally making the home a museum to be endured rather than enjoyed.

In our hands we literally have the making, or marring, of a home. We can let the house rule us, or vice versa. I find that turning a blind eye to the housework sometimes, such as occasionally during school holidays, relieves the monotony of the daily round of chores, and afterwards brings me back to it with more enthusiasm to tackle what I had left undone.

There is a happy medium in all things; housework, in my opinion, is no exception.

DON'T THROW IT AWAY

TURNING out drawers and cupboards during spring cleaning very often leaves us with a pile of items which are better than junk and too good to throw away. Unless a jumble sale comes along about the same time, we are left wondering how to dispose of the lot?

The gift shops opened by Oxfam and other organisations in several Westcountry towns provide one answer. They will gratefully receive such saleable things as clothes, toys, books, records, china, and bric-a-brac.

The W.R.V.S. and Salvation Army are thankful for men and women's clothes, and Oxfam can always do with oddments of knitting wool for making up into blanket squares.

The welfare department of your local authority might well be interested in furniture which they could use for re-housing a needy person, and the Simon Community Centre in Exeter have need of mattresses, sheets, and blankets.

Don't throw these items away — someone might need them! Write to me if you would like further names and addresses.

POSTSCRIPT ON BREAD-MAKING

DURING the Easter school holiday my children wanted to try their hand at bread-making. They mixed their yeasty liquid, left it hanging around till it became quite cold, then hurriedly put it into the warm again. Once more it started to froth, and they poured the liquid on to 1lb. plain flour and had great fun trying to get the resulting sticky mess from their fingers.

They used the dough as plasticine, rolled and pummelled it into balls and other odd shapes, slapped it all on to a baking sheet, and pleaded for it to be baked.

I quite expected hard lumps of clay to emerge from the oven, but not only did the rolls (a very loose term !) look good but they tasted as nice as any bread I had made with the utmost care and precision regarding times and temperature. It's just not fair!

This article was written by Lord Clinton (Gerard Fane-Trefusis, the 22nd baron Clinton). The article appeared in the Western Times on Friday 18th April 1969. Two of Lord Clinton's children attended Alice's school during the 1960s.

A rather amusing story was told to me by Mrs Kathleen Harris which relates to the article on the previous page. Apparently only a week or so before the article appeared in the paper, Kath had approached Alice asking whether she could put a little piece in the paper about her school and retirement, as Kath was the local correspondent at the time for 'The Western Times.' Alice made it quite clear that in no way did she want anything to appear in the paper. Kath gracefully accepted Alice's decision and no more was said. However, when Alice opened the paper a couple of weeks later, she nearly blew her top as she read the heading "BROKEN ARM ENDS OVER 50 YEARS OF TEACHING.", and found that it was all about her. To add insult to injury, not just that her wish had been ignored, the article stated that Alice was "over 80", when in actual fact she was seventy-seven. Alice was then on the war path, and when she next encountered Kath, poor Kath's life was hardly worth living. She had some trouble in trying to convince Alice it was not her who had written the article. When Alice discovered that it was Lord Clinton who wrote the article, then it didn't seem quite so bad after all. Thankfully all ended happily, with Alice apologising to Kath.

Alice's broken arm was the result of a fall in her own home. It was Jack Mardon who found her on the floor by the fireplace, in a pool of blood, having knocked her head in the fall. Alice was duly sent to hospital and received medical attention. After she was sent home, she had to accept that her teaching career was over. Kathleen also persuaded Alice that she could no longer carry on teaching. Alice felt annoyed and frustrated about the whole situation. Retirement was certainly not her preferred option. However, she didn't do badly when one considers she was seventy-six when she finally 'hung up her hat'. It is just as well that she did retire, as some people recall that she was beginning to get short tempered and a little impatient with her pupils, not always having the absolute control that she once had. Even so, her mind remained very active through her retirement, and she often helped children who wanted extra tuition with forthcoming exams. During those last years, Alice received many letters, as well as regular visits, from former pupils, which was always of great enjoyment to her.

Then in December of 1972, Alice had a stroke and was taken into Bideford Hospital, but from then on she gradually deteriorated. On hearing the news, there were many in the community who were concerned about her, and had expressed their desire to Kathleen Wadland that they wished to visit Alice, but Kathleen said that Alice didn't want or was in any fit state to receive visitors. Although she was seriously ill, Alice was certainly not beyond having some callers and couldn't understand the lack of them, whereupon some friends who had ignored Kathleen's request, called in to see Alice, and the truth soon became apparent. Alice was greatly upset as she had made no such request. We can only assume that Kathleen was simply acting in an over-protective manner, and greatly concerned for her sister's well-being. However, Alice did not recover, and she died without any of her family or friends by her bedside on 27th December 1972. Thus ended the life of an amazing individual. Even Kathleen* and the remaining sisters admitted that none of them could ever step into Alice's shoes. A unique era had well and truly ended.

*Kathleen died in 1977, and was buried with Alice, in Dolton churchyard; Margaret became blind, and died in Reading hospital, in 1980; Elsie died a widow in Sussex in 1982; and dear old Winifred died in a residential home in Blackpool in 1983.

A TRUE DOLTONIAN
AND A COMMON ANCESTRY

My connection with Alice is one of kinship, as I descend from another line of Wadlands, who in the last century left Great Venton in Dolton and moved to Cornwall. Alice and I share the same forebears through John and Sarah Wadland, who as a young married couple moved to Dolton (c 1782), and rented Ashwell Farm from the Furse family before inheriting property of their own.

Having such a long association with Dolton, Alice naturally felt very much at home, and theoretically was a true Doltonian herself. Likewise, although I was not born and bred in the parish, I am very proud of my own deeply engrained alliances with Dolton.

Alice and her siblings all died without issue. The only person who married was the youngest, Elsie, but there were no children. It's sad to think that this whole branch of the family has died out. However, all was assuredly not lost when you consider what they gave to society, and the one who gave the most was of course Our Miss Wadland.

INDEX OF PUPILS
1917 - 1968

INDEX OF PUPILS
1917 - 1968
CONTINUED.

INDEX OF PUPILS
1917 - 1968
CONTINUED.

76. Heal, Isabel	1941 - 1947
77. Heal, Jean	1940 - 1943
78. Heal, John	1942 - 1947
79. Heal, Rosemary	1940 - 1942
80. Heaman, A	1936 (just 3 days)
81. Heaman, Margaret	1923 - 1936
82. Heard, Mildred	1941 - 1943
83. Hockin, Joan	1940 - 1942
84. Holwill, Cecilia	1940 - 1948
85. Holwill, Mary	1937 - 1944
86. Holwill, Nancy	1925 - 1933
87. Holwill, Owen	1937 - 1940
88. Hooper, Mabel	
89. Hooper, Mary	
90. Hooper, Ruth	
91. Hooper, Ruth	
92. Hopper, Ann	1946 - 1947
93. Hopper, Richard	1946 - 1951
94. Hunt, Gillian	1938 - 1939
95. Hunt, Moira	1938 - 1940
96. Hutchings, Hannah Katherine	1917 - 1924
97. Kirswell, Christopher	1966 (1 term)
98. Leatt, Charmaine	1964 - 1968
99. Leatt, Gabrielle	1960 - 1966
100. Lee, Juliet Maud	1955 - 1956
101. Lemon, Irene	1917 - 1919
102. Lendon, Ruth	1944 - 1947
103. Lister, Jill	1946 - 1952
104. Lomas, Peter	1950 - (2 terms)
105. Luxton, Frances	1917- 1924 (approx)
106. Lynch-Blosse, David	1931 - 1934*
107. Lynch-Blosse, Sylvia	1934 - 1941
108 .Martin, Hazel	1940 - 1943
109. May, Helen	1965 - 1968
110. May, Michael	1966 - 1968
111. May, Roger	1968 (1 term)
112. Maynard, Jean	1947 - 1953

*1st boy pupil

INDEX OF PUPILS
1917 - 1968
CONTINUED.

INDEX OF PUPILS
1917 - 1968
CONTINUED.

150.	Stoneman, Kathleen	c. 1929
151.	Tabor, Roger	1949 - 1952
152.	Taylor, Caroline	1964 (1 term)
153.	Taylor, Christopher	1964 (1 term)
154.	Thomas, Elsie	1918 (2 terms)
155.	Tillbrook, Ann	1946 - 1949
156.	Trick, Molly	1931 - 1932
157.	Turrall, Diane	1941 - 1944
158.	Turrall, Richard	1943 - 1945
159.	Underhill, Angela	1960 - 1966
160.	Underhill, Mary	1957 - 1963
161.	Underhill, Michael	1964 - 1968
162.	Vosper, Anthony	1950 - 1954
163.	Vosper, John	1949 - 1950
164.	Walford, Hazel	1940 - 1941
165.	Walker, David	1960 - 1963
166.	Walker, Penelope (Penny)	1962 -1963
167.	Watkins, Violet	1931 - 1934
168.	Way, Richard	1946 (2 terms)
169.	Weeks, Michael	1957 - 1961
170.	Weeks, Tony	1946 - 1947
171.	West, Colin	1951 - 1956
172.	West, David	1952 - 1957
173.	West, Nicholas	1948 - 1952
174.	West, Pricilla	1954 - 1959
175.	Westcott, Diana	1945 - 1948
176.	Whistler, Simon Laurence	1948 - 1950
177.	Williams, Joyce	1947 - 1951
178.	Williams, Roger	1947 - 1948
179.	Wills, David	1955 - 1957
180.	Winfield, Ailsa	1958 - 1959
181.	Winfield, Johnathon	1959 - 1959
182.	Winifred, Lucille	1959 (1 term)
183.	Wood, Gloria	1940 - 1942

During the last stages of completing this book I was absolutely delighted to be told by Derek Mardon that he had found Alice's school registers while sorting out his parents' possessions. For the past twelve years I have been searching for the registers, and virtually by the time of finishing this book I had given up all hope of ever locating them, coming to the conclusion that they must have been thrown away after the contents clearance of Alice's property in 1975. Once again, thankfully, it was due to Jack and Mabel Mardon's foresight for having retrieved the registers together with other papers relating to the school. The reason why the letters were destroyed was because at the time they were regarded as being private, and of no use to anyone outside the family. In April 1998, Derek Mardon very kindly gave me the registers to keep and in turn I will eventually give them to the record office as part of their archives. Initially when I started writing this book I had to build up my own index of Alice's pupils, and had acquired approximately one hundred and sixty-seven names. When finally obtaining the registers I was able to add another twenty names, so I felt rather satisfied by the work I had done in building an index from scratch, although the original registers were extremely helpful in clarifying the exact dates/years that the pupils attended the school.

∞∞∞∞

There has been great difficulty in obtaining any proven evidence of Alice's life from the autumn of 1908 to the end of 1914. It is most probable that when Alice finished her own schooling at Badminton, in the summer of 1908, she entered some University College in the autumn of 1908 to start training for her chosen career. I have been in contact with Badminton School, only to be told that they have no records covering the relevant period. The elusive years make it difficult to ascertain exactly what Alice's professional status was, as nothing conclusive has come to light as to whether or not she was a member of any society. It is known however, that Alice's sister Winifred was a member of The Royal Society of Teachers which was abolished in 1949. There was also The College of Preceptors (founded in

1849), and it is very likely (according to Richard Willis, formerly of Cambridge University) that Alice at some stage during her career was a member of this particular society, but it should be emphasised that it was not compulsory for practitioners to register.

One person I missed by about a year was Violet Dalby, (nee Hare), having died in 1989. As previously mentioned Alice was a private governess to Violet from 1915 to 1917, and with their lifelong association, it's almost certain that Violet would have known something about Alice's early career. Also I was rather surprised by Roger Page's (former pupil) comments that when he visited Alice about a year before her death, she told him that she had taught over 300 children. initially this threw me into utter confusion, however, once the school registers came to light, I was soon able to see exactly how many pupils she had, and the number came to 187, plus Violet, making 188. Therefore, I can only suggest that to account for the approximate 112 unknown pupils, Alice possibly taught in a private school, somewhere from the autumn of 1911 to the end of 1914. Nonetheless, I am still inclined to think that this didn't actually occur, and that there was some misunderstanding between Alice and Roger during their conversation, I think it far more likely that when Alice finished some form of University College training, she went into the employment of some aristocratic/gentry family, and then continued this form of employment with the Hare family of Diptford. To further substantiate this theory, if you refer to Alice's obituary (page 141), it clearly states that when she began teaching, it was in the form of 'visiting pupils' (which then was the more usual form of employment), and no mention of teaching in a private school. The main contributor of the obituary was Kathleen Wadland.

On the next page is a graph showing the officially registered children for each month, covering the years from 1917 to 1968. Unfortunately, the current whereabouts of the register from 1917 to the end of the summer term of 1924 is not known, and I have substituted this period with my own approximate calculations.

The following grid quotes (per month) the officially registered pupils at Alice Wadland's private school. The figures were extracted from the original school registers which are now in the possession of the author.

	JAN	FEB	MAR	APR	MAY	JUN	JUL	AUG	SEP	OCT	NOV	DEC
1917	—	—	—	—	—	—	—	—	8	8	8	8
1918	8	8	8	8	8	8	8	—	11	11	11	11
1919	10	10	10	10	10	10	10	—	7	7	7	7
1920	7	7	7	7	7	7	7	—	7	7	7	8
1921	8	8	8	8	8	8	8	—	9	9	9	9
1922	10	10	10	10	10	10	10	—	10	10	10	10
1923	9	9	9	9	9	9	9	—	9	9	9	9
1924	7	7	7	7	7	7	7	—	9	9	9	9
1925	6	6	6	6	6	6	6	-	6	6	6	6
1926	6	6	6	6	6	6	6	-	6	6	6	6
1927	5	5	5	5	6	6	?	-	?	?	?	?
1928	?	?	?	?	?	?	?	-	?	?	?	?
1929	?	?	?	?	?	?	?	-	?	?	?	?
1930	?	?	?	?	?	?	?	-	6	7	7	7
1931	6	6	6	8	8	8	7	-	9	9	9	9
1932	9	9	9	8	8	8	8	-	8	8	8	8
1933	8	8	8	8	6	6	5	-	6	6	6	6
1934	6	6	6	6	5	5	5	-	4	4	4	4
1935	4	4	4	4	4	4	4	-	4	4	4	4
1936	4	4	4	4	3	3	3	-	2	2	2	2
1937	2	2	2	4	4	4	3	-	4	4	4	4
1938	4	4	4	4	7	7	5	-	3	4	3	3
1939	3	3	3	3	3	3	3	-	7	7	7	7
1940	5	5	5	5	5	5	6	-	8	9	10	9
1941	12	12	12	12	12	12	12	-	14	14	14	13
1942	13	13	13	13	14	13	13	-	11	11	11	11
1943	13	13	13	13	15	15	15	-	14	14	16	15
1944	15	16	16	16	16	16	16	-	16	15	15	15
1945	15	15	15	15	15	15	15	-	16	16	16	16
1946	17	17	17	17	17	17	17	-	15	15	15	15
1947	15	15	15	10	10	10	10	-	12	12	12	11
1948	10	10	10	12	14	14	13	-	11	11	11	11
1949	11	11	11	11	13	13	13	-	14	14	14	14
1950	16	16	16	15	14	14	14	-	14	14	14	14
1951	14	14	14	14	15	15	15	-	13	13	13	13
1952	13	13	13	13	15	15	15	-	13	13	13	13
1953	15	15	15	15	16	16	16	-	15	15	15	15
1954	14	15	15	15	17	17	17	-	16	16	16	16
1955	16	16	16	16	16	16	16	-	15	15	14	14
1956	14	14	14	14	14	14	14	-	14	14	14	14
1957	17	17	17	17	17	17	17	-	14	14	16	16
1958	15	15	15	15	16	16	16	-	16	16	16	16
1959	17	17	17	17	17	17	17	-	15	15	14	16
1960	14	14	14	14	14	14	14	-	14	15	15	15
1961	16	16	16	17	17	15	15	-	13	13	13	13
1962	14	14	14	14	14	14	14	-	15	15	15	15
1963	15	15	15	15	15	13	13	-	9	9	9	9
1964	9	9	9	10	10	10	10	-	13	15	15	15
1965	14	14	14	14	14	14	14	-	15	15	15	15
1966	16	16	16	16	16	16	16	-	15	15	15	15
1967	14	14	14	16	16	16	16	-	12	12	12	12
1968	12	12	12	12	15	15	15	-	11	11	11	*

*The school's sudden closure occurred on Monday 4th November, 1968. This was due to Alice breaking her arm, from a fall, and this forced her into retirement,, but much to her reluctance.

Pages from one of the school's registers, covering part of 1927, the whole of 1928 and 1929, and the 1st two terms of 1930, are unfortunately missing.

DOLTON LOSES
A FRIEND

Dolton has lost a friend and personality by the death in Bideford Hospital, at the age of 80, of Miss Alice Mary Wadland.

Miss Wadland, who lived at Southover, had for about 60 years taught privately, first going to visit pupils and later at her own school, and she is remembered with affection by all her old pupils.

She officially retired in the autumn of 1968, but even since then she has given individual attention to children anxious to pass their O-level examinations, observing "I want to keep my brain active."

FORMER PUPILS

What gave her particular pleasure in her retirement were the many letters she received from former pupils now living all over the world.

Children from all walks of life benefited from her instruction. In many instances she had taught two generations of the same family.

For 49 years she had been organist at the Parish Church.

Born at Owlacombe, Roborough, she was the fifth of a family of seven there.

Her brother Henry Lawrence, eldest of the family, lost his life in the First World War. Of the sisters Mary died young, Winifred now lives in Lancashire, Kathleen (who was teaching English and French at the age of 16) in Dolton, Margaret in Berkshire, and Elsie Hannah (Mrs. E. H. Morris, a widow) in Sussex.

The Wadland family left Roborough for Langport, where they lived for 15 years before returning to Dolton district to take up residence at Arscotts, where Miss Wadland first began her teaching.

In her younger days Miss Wadland was the organiser of the local Girls' Friendly Society; and she allowed the young people of the village the use of her tennis court, and was a keen tennis player herself.

The funeral of Miss Wadland took place last week at Dolton Parish Church, the Rector, Rev. F. R. Morse, officiating. Lay reader Mr. D. J. V. Davies read the lesson.

Many friends, including former pupils, attended.

Her sister, Miss K. Wadland, was the principal mourner present.

Bearers were Messrs C. Fishleigh, J. Mardon, D. J. Mardon and M. Turner.

Obituary which appeared in the North Devon Journal

Dolton.

Personalia—Alice Mary Wadland. This month
we record the passing of one of our most respected residents. She was very well known, not only
in the parish, but over quite a wide area because of
her very successful school where she taught for
over sixty years. We especially remember her as
a faithful and loyal member of our Church, she
was our Organist for forty nine years, in addition,
she organised the Flower Rota and the decorating
at Festival times was carried out under her super-
vision. We thank God for her life and witness and
offer our sincere sympathy to all relatives and
friends.   F.R.M.

The above was written by the Rev Frank Moorse, who was
rector of Dolton and Dowland form 1963 to 1979. The personalia appeared in the February issue of the Torrington
Deanery Magazine. Frank Moorse had very happy memories of Alice, and in his own words; "She was a wonderful
lady, and I had the greatest of respect for her. Alice was a
deeply committed Christian, and as well as being a regular
communicant at St Edmond's, she and her sister Kathleen
also attended Dowland Church."
In 1993 I had the pleasure of meeting Frank Moorse at a
small lunch party in Dolton. He had virtually lost his eyesight, and I remember when I was introduced to him, he
said in a rather loud voice "Pleased to meet you sir, are you
retired?" This caused much laughter in the room. I said to
him "No, I'm not, however I wish I was." I then told him I
was only in my late twenties. For some reason he seemed
rather amazed that anyone 'so young' should be writing the
life story of Miss Wadland.

EDUCATIONAL CHARGES
A SUMMARY

Most of the charges in the grid on p144 are accurate. The period over which there is some doubt is the 1950s, so approximate costs have been substituted. For the first ten years of establishing her school Alice charged £4.10 shillings a term. Then in the Christmas term of 1926, her rate went up to £5.10 shillings. This rate remained static until the Christmas term of 1939, when on the outbreak of World War II, Alice dropped her rate back to £4.10 shillings. Although this was a drop of £1 a term, per pupil, she was well compensated for the fact that her class size had more than doubled in 1940, which included evacuee children. The rate remained the same until 1943 when Alice dropped the rate another 6 shillings to £4. 4 shillings, and then in 1944 there was a further reduction to £3.11 shillings a term, and this rate remained the same for the whole year. The reason for Alice dropping the rate to the 1944 level was that she felt that she had to make a personal sacrifice as part of the war effort. However, in the following year her rate went back up to £4.4s a term, and this stayed in effect until the end of 1946. At the beginning of 1947 the rate went up to £5.5s a term, and this then changed in the Easter term of 1953 to £7.17s.6d. In the Christmas term of 1955 the rate went up to £8 a term and then in the Christmas term of 1958, it went up to £10 a term, and finally in the Christmas term of 1961, the rate was increased to £12. This charge remained the same until the closure of the school in 1968. For the period 1917 to the summer term of 1963, Alice's rates for boarders was approximately double to that which was paid by the day pupils. However, on the whole, exact costs of what boarders paid are rather scant as Alice wouldn't take more than two or three boarders at any one time and there were periods when she didn't have any at all.

APPROX COST OF EDUCATION PER TERM FOR DAY PUPILS

YEAR	EASTER TERM			SUMMER TERM			CHRISTMAS TERM		
	£.	s.	d.	£.	s.	d.	£.	s.	d.
1917	---	---	---	---	---	---	4	10	00
1918	4	10	00	4	10	00	4	10	00
1919	4	10	00	4	10	00	4	10	00
1920	4	10	00	4	10	00	4	10	00
1921	4	10	00	4	10	00	4	10	00
1922	4	10	00	4	10	00	4	10	00
1923	4	10	00	4	10	00	4	10	00
1924	4	10	00	4	10	00	4	10	00
1925	4	10	00	4	10	00	4	10	00
1926	4	10	10	4	10	00	5	10	00
1927	5	10	00	5	10	00	5	10	00
1928	5	10	00	5	10	00	5	10	00
1929	5	10	00	5	10	00	5	10	00
1930	5	10	00	5	10	00	5	10	00
1931	5	10	00	5	10	00	5	10	00
1932	5	10	00	5	10	00	5	10	00
1933	5	10	00	5	10	00	5	10	00
1934	5	10	00	5	10	00	5	10	00
1935	5	10	00	5	10	00	5	10	00
1936	5	10	00	5	10	00	5	10	00
1937	5	10	00	5	10	00	5	10	00
1938	5	10	00	5	10	00	5	10	00
1939	5	10	00	5	10	00	4	10	00
1940	4	10	00	4	10	00	4	10	00
1941	4	10	00	4	10	00	4	10	00
1942	4	10	00	4	10	00	4	10	00
1943	4	4	00	4	4	00	4	4	00
1944	3	11	00	3	11	00	3	11	00
1945	4	4	00	4	4	00	4	4	00
1946	4	4	00	4	4	00	4	4	00
1947	5	5	00	5	5	00	5	5	00
1948	5	5	00	5	5	00	5	5	00
1949	5	5	00	5	5	00	5	5	00
1950	5	5	00	5	5	00	5	5	00
1951	5	5	00	5	5	00	5	5	00
1952	5	5	00	5	5	00	5	00	00
1953	7	17	6	7	17	6	7	17	6
1954	7	17	6	7	17	6	7	17	6
1955	7	17	6	7	17	6	8	00	00
1956	8	00	00	8	00	00	8	00	00
1957	8	00	00	8	00	00	8	00	00
1958	8	00	00	8	00	00	10	00	00
1959	10	00	00	10	00	00	10	00	00
1960	10	00	00	10	00	00	10	00	00
1961	10	00	00	10	00	00	12	00	00
1962	12	00	00	12	00	00	12	00	00
1963	12	00	00	12	00	00	12	00	00
1964	12	00	00	12	00	00	12	00	00
1965	12	00	00	12	00	00	12	00	00
1966	12	00	00	12	00	00	12	00	00
1967	12	00	00	12	00	00	12	00	00
1968	12	00	00	12	00	00	12	00	00

APPROX COST PER TERM FOR BOARDERS

YEAR	EASTER TERM £.	s.	d.	SUMMER TERM £.	s.	d.	CHRISTMAS TERM £.	s.	d.
1917	----------			----------			8	8	00
1918	8	8	00	8	8	00	8	8	00
1919	8	8	00	8	8	00	8	8	00
1920	8	8	00	8	8	00	8	8	00
1921	8	8	00	8	8	00	8	8	00
1922	8	8	00	8	8	00	8	8	00
1923	8	8	00	8	8	00	8	8	00
1924	8	8	00	8	8	00	8	8	00
1925	8	8	00	8	8	00	8	8	00
1926	8	8	00	8	8	00	8	8	00
1927	8	8	00	8	8	00	8	8	00
1928	8	8	00	8	8	00	8	8	00
1929	8	8	00	8	8	00	8	8	00
1930	8	8	00	8	8	00	8	8	00
1931	8	8	00	8	8	00	8	8	00
1932	8	8	00	8	8	00	8	8	00
1933	8	8	00	8	8	00	8	8	00
1934	8	8	00	8	8	00	8	8	00
1935	8	8	00	8	8	00	8	8	00
1936	8	8	00	8	8	00	8	8	00
1937	8	8	00	8	8	00	8	8	00
1938	8	8	00	8	8	00	8	8	00
1939	8	8	00	8	8	00	Rate possibly dropped		
1940	?			?			?		
1941	?			?			?		
1942	?			?			?		
1943	?			?			?		
1944	8	8	00	8	8	00	8	8	00
1945	8	8	00	8	8	00	8	8	00
1946	8	8	00	8	8	00	8	8	00
1947	8	8	00	8	8	00	8	8	00
1948	8	8	00	8	8	00	8	8	00
1949	?			?			?		
1950	?			?			?		
1951	?			?			?		
1952	?			?			?		
1953	14	00	00	14	00	00	14	00	00
1954	14	00	00	14	00	00	14	00	00
1955	14	00	00	14	00	00	14	00	00
1956	14	00	00	14	00	00	14	00	00
1957	?			?			?		
1958	?			?			?		
1959	?			?			?		
1960	?			?			?		
1961	?			?			?		
1962	?			?			?		
1963	?			?			----------		

During the summer holiday of 1963, Alice moved from Sages to Southover, and discontinued having boarders. When the school re-opened in the Christmas Term of 1963, Alice then ran her establishment as a preparatory school, with children leaving Southover when they attained the ages of 9 or 10.

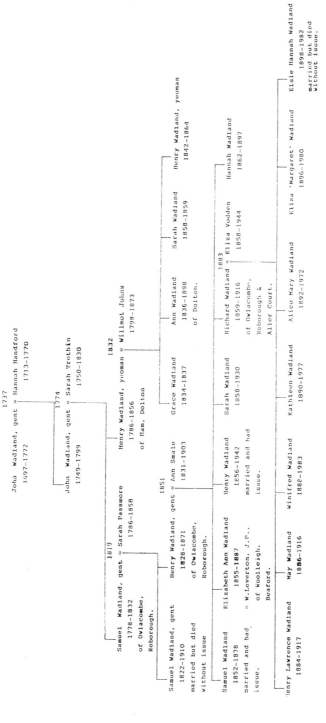

1737
John Wadland, gent = Hannah Handford
1697-1772   1713-1770

1774
John Wadland, gent = Sarah Trothin
1749-1799   1750-1830

1832
Henry Wadland, yeoman = Willmot Johns
1786-1856   1798-1873
of Ham, Dolton

1819
Samuel Wadland, gent = Sarah Passmore
1778-1832   1786-1858
of Owlacombe,
Roborough.

Samuel Wadland, gent
1822-1910
married but died
without issue

Henry Wadland, gent = Ann Seale
1828-1871   1831-1903
of Owlacombe,
Roborough.   1851

Grace Wadland
1834-1837

Ann Wadland
1836-1898
of Dolton.

Sarah Wadland
1858-1859

Henry Wadland, yeoman
1842-1864

Samuel Wadland
1852-1878
married and had
issue.

Elizabeth Ann Wadland
1855-1887
= W.Leverton, J.P.,
of Woolleigh,
Beaford.

Henry Wadland
1856-1942
married and had
issue.

Sarah Wadland
1858-1930

Richard Wadland = Eliza Vodden
1859-1916   1858-1944
of Owlacombe,   1883
Roborough &
Aller Court.

Hannah Wadland
1862-1897

Henry Lawrence Wadland
1884-1917

May Wadland
1886-1916

Winifred Wadland
1888-1983

Kathleen Wadland
1890-1977

Alice Mary Wadland
1892-1972

Eliza 'Margaret' Wadland
1896-1980

Elsie Hannah Wadland
1898-1982
married but died
without issue.

OBITUARY

ROBOROUGH

The funeral of Mr Richard Wadland took place in the family burial ground at Roborough. Deceased was 57 years of age and had been a successful agriculturist formerly at Roborough, and latterly at Langport, Somerset. During the prime of life he occupied public offices, and was deeply interested in public business. His opinion and experience were sought. The funeral was largely attended. The coffin was born by motor hearse to Roborough. The Rector (the Rev. T. Barnard) officiated. The chief mourners were the widow and five daughters, Mr S Wadland (brother), Miss S Wadland (sister), Mrs S Wadland (sister-in-law), Mr Leverton J.P. (brother-in-law) and Messrs W H Leverton and A Leverton (nephews). The bearers were Messrs Quick and Woods (tenants), Blackmore, Maynard, Squance and Thomas. The motor hearse and funeral cars were supplied by Mr J Dillin, Dolton.

RICHARD WADLAND
1859 - 1916

OBITUARY

ROBOROUGH

The funeral took place on Saturday, amid every token of sympathy and respect, of Miss May Wadland, daughter of Mr & Mrs R Wadland of Arscotts, Dolton, and late of Langport, Somerset and Owlacombe, Roborough (North Devon). The deceased passed away at a nursing home in South Devon. The body was encased in a coffin of unpolished oak, the brass shield bearing the inscription: "May Wadland died Jan 4th 1916 aged 30 years." The remains were conveyed from South Devon to Roborough by motor, and were interred in the family burial ground on the south side of the Parish Church. There was a very large attendance of relatives and friends, the bereaved family being widely known and much respected. The bearers were tenants and old workmen on the estate. The hymn "Peace, perfect peace" was sung in the church. The Rector (Rev. T. Barnard) officiated. A large number of beautiful floral tributes were laid on the grave. The funeral motor and mourning car were supplied by Mr J Dillin, Dolton.

MAY WADLAND
Born 7th June 1886, Died 5th January 1916.

THE WILL OF ANN WADLAND

This is the last Will and Testament of me Ann Wadland of the parish of Dolton in the county of Devon, spinster.

I give unto Samuel Wadland of the parish of Braunton in the county of Devon his executors and administrators all of that tenement and farm called or known by the name of Chapel Mill Down and all other my lands in the parish of Winkleigh in the County of Devon upon trust that is to say to permit and suffer my cousin Mary Ann Johns of the parish of Dolton, spinster, to receive the rents and profits thereof for her own use and benefit during the term of her natural life.

I give all the above mentioned tenement known by the name of Chapel Mill Down and all other my lands in the parish of Winkleigh unto Sarah Wadland daughter of my late cousin Henry Wadland of the parish of Roborough and Hannah Marguerita Leverton daughter of William and Elizabeth Ann Leverton of the parish of Beaford in equal shares as tenants in common and their respective heirs administrators and assigns for ever but subject nevertheless to the life interest of the said Mary Ann Johns as before mentioned. And is the said Mary Ann Johns should happen to die before the said Hannah Marguerita Leverton attains the age of twenty one years then in that event I appoint the said Sarah Wadland and William Leverton as trustees to receive the portion of the rent and profits of the said estate and to allow the same to accumulate during her minority but if she should happen to die before attaining the age of twenty one years then I give her portion of the said estate together with the accumulations (if any) in equal shares between her two brothers William Henry and Arthur Leverton their respective heirs and assigns for ever. I give unto my cousin the said Samuel Wadland the legacy of fifteen pounds. I give unto my cousin William Johns of the parish of Dolton, carpenter, the sum of one hundred pounds. I give unto each of my first cousins (except Samuel Wadland Mary Ann Johns and William Johns before mentioned) who shall be living in England at the time of my decease the sum of ten pounds. I give unto Henry Wadland of Avon Bassett Warwickshire the sum of ten pounds. I give unto each of the daughters of my late cousin Hannah Madge and Thomas Acland Madge of the parish of Meeth the sum of twenty pounds. I give unto Thomas Acland Madge, the son of my late cousin Hannah Madge and Thomas Acland Madge of the parish of Meeth the sum of five pounds. I give unto Mrs Ann Wadland widow of my late cousin Henry Wadland of Roborough the sum of five pounds. I give to the Society for the propagation of the Gospel in Foreign Parts the sum of twenty pounds to be applied to the purposes of the Society and a receipt of a Treasurer of the Society shall be a sufficient discharge for the same. I give unto the Devon House of Mercy at Bovey Tracey the sum of twenty pounds to be paid to one of the Treasurers out of such part of my personal estate as I can lawfully charge with it. I give unto the North Devon Infirmary at Barnstaple the sum of twenty pounds to be paid to one of the Treasurers out of such part of my personal estate as I can lawfully charge with it. I give unto the Additional Curates Society the sum of twenty pounds to be paid out of such part of my personal estate as I can lawfully charge with it to be applied to the purposes of the Society and a receipt of a Treasurer of the said Society shall be a sufficient discharge for the same I leave my house in which I reside in the village of Dolton to the Rector of Dolton and his successors in trust to pay the rents thereof to the use of the National School in the parish of Dolton so long as it continues to be a National School and afterwards in trust for expenses connected with the Sunday School the accounts to be annually audited by the Churchwardens. I leave all the books in the bookcase in the kitchen also the bookcase in the kitchen and all the other books which have usually been lent out to the Rector of Dolton and his successors in trust for a parish library. I leave all my clothes and furniture except the bookcase before mentioned, to my cousin Mary Ann Johns and I also request that she should be allowed to reside in the house in which I reside at present for the space of one year rent free I direct that all the above mentioned legacies shall be paid within twelve months next after my decease as to all the rest residue and remainder of my real and personal estate and all of property of what nature or kind soever (except what is before mentioned) I give devise and bequeath the same unto Richard Wadland son of my late cousin Henry Wadland of the parish of Roborough his heirs executors administrators and assigns but subject to the payment of my just debts testamentary and funeral expenses and the legacies hereinbefore given and I hereby appoint the said Richard Wadland sole Executor of this my Will in Witness whereof I have hereunto set my hand this fourth day of January one thousand eight hundred and ninety eight the words "and after the decease of the" having been previously erased opposite our initials – ANN WADLAND – SIGNED by the said Testatrix as her last Will and Testament in the presence of us present at the same time who at her request in her presence and in the presence of each other have subscribed our names as witnesses – AP DRUMMOND MD of Dolton N Devon. – AM DRUMMOND of N Devon

On the 9th day of February 1898 Probate of this Will was granted to Richard Wadland the sole Executor.

THE WILL OF ALICE WADLAND

This is the last Will & Testament of me Alice Mary Wadland of "Southover" Dolton, Winkleigh in the county of Devon, Spinster...

1. I revoke all prior testamentary writings and appoint Lloyds Bank Limited (hereinafter called "the Bank") to be the executor and trustee of this my Will, and I declare that the Bank's terms and conditions for acting as executor and trustee (including the scale of remuneration) last published before the date of my death shall apply with power to charge remuneration in accordance with any later published terms of the Bank for the time being in force. I approve of Messrs W H Stone and Company of 6 Northernhay Place in the county of the City of Exeter being employed as Solicitors in connection with my estate with power for the Bank to consult any other Solicitor(s) if it thinks fit...

2. I devise my property known as "Southover" aforesaid (formerly known as Rose Cottage) and bequeath all the contents therein – excluding money or securities for money – to my sister Miss Kathleen Wadland of "Southover" aforesaid free of all duties.

3. I make the following bequests free of all duties:
  a) To my said sister Kathleen Wadland a legacy of Three hundred pounds.
  b) To my sister Miss Winifred Wadland of 33 Rodney Street Liverpool, a legacy of Seven hundred pounds and my Two hundred and eighty six pounds Thirteen shillings and Four pence three and one half per centum Treasury Stock (British Iron and Steel).
  c) To my sister Miss Eliza Margaret Wadland of 275 Wykeham Road Earley Reading Berkshire my One thousand and seventy four pounds Eleven shillings and Ten pence four per centum Consols and a legacy of Seven hundred pounds.
  d) To my sister Mrs Elsie Hannah Morris of 23 Pelham Road Worthing Sussex a legacy of Seven hundred pounds and my Three hundred and seven pounds Eighteen shillings and four pence three and one half per centum War Stock (Registered).

4. I bequeath my National Savings Certificates to my said four sisters in equal shares free of all duties.

5. I devise and bequeath all the residue of my estate of whatsoever description and wheresoever situate to the Bank Upon Trust to sell and convert the same into money and upon further trust to

divide the net proceeds of such sale and conversion equally between my four sisters.

In witness whereof I have hereto set my hand this sixteenth day of September One thousand nine hundred and sixty seven.
Alice Mary Wadland

Signed by the said Alice Mary Wadland the Testatrix as and for her last Will and Testament in the presence of us both present at the same time who at her request in her presence and in the presence of each other have hereto subscribed our names as witnesses

Ada Aletta Ethel Annie Piper   John Mardon
West Lane Dolton   Roselea
Housewife   Dolton
       Postman

Will proved Bristol 11th March 1973.

INDEX

INDEX

INDEX

AMW

LIST OF SUBSCRIBERS

A

Mrs Kathleen Adams – Northam, Devon
Ruth Arnold – Nethercott, Iddesleigh

B

Paul and Simon Berry – Beaford, Devon
Sarah Bell, nee Pickard – Barnstaple, Devon
Roger and Enid Brown – Exbourne, Devon
Henry Banbury – Iddesleigh, Devon
John and Margaret Bailey – Albaston, Gunnislake, Cornwall
Andrea Byrne – Dolton, Devon
Mrs Jill Buckingham – Dolton, Devon
Mrs Margaret Brimacombe – Dolton, Devon

C

Mrs Emmi Cockram – Dolton, Devon
Peter and Pamela Cantle – Instow, Devon
Cecilia M Cameron – Iddesleigh, Devon
Joan Cullen – Crowlink, Sussex
Henry Chapman – Torrington, Devon
Shane and Gail (nee Wadland) Cox – Tamworth, N.S.W, Australia
Andrew and Nicky Coombe – Callington, Cornwall
Simon Chivers – Dolton, Devon
The Right Honourable Lord and Lady Clinton

D

Mrs Mary Dunn – Cheriton Fitzpaine, Devon

F

David and Miriam Fitter – Dolton, Devon
Miss B Friend – Dolton, Devon
Leslie and Betty Friend – Wadland Barton, Ashbury, Devon
Nicola Fleming – Bishop's Stortford, Herts
Keith and Adrienne Farmer – Dolton, Devon
The Honourable Charles Fane-Trefusis – Colaton Raleigh, Devon
The Hon. Mrs Fowle – Heanton Satchville, Devon
Maralin Fraser – Broadhempston, Devon
Mrs M Fishleigh – Dolton, Devon

G

Kenneth and Mary Goodman – Launceston, Cornwall
June Grigg – Okehampton, Devon
Rosemary Guard – Dolton, Devon
Mary Gent – Dowland, Devon

H

Ann Hopper, nee Blakeley – Whitby, Ontario, Canada
Mrs Kathleen Hawkey MBE – Wantage, Oxon
Christopher John Hawkey – The Park, Nottingham
Kate Hawkey – Bishopston, Bristol
Lorna Hodge, nee Wadland – Werribee, Victoria, Australia
Mrs Hilary Hadden – Exeter, Devon
Diana Hurst, nee Bonham – Plymouth, Devon
Sue Hyne – Dolton, Devon
Rosemary Heal – Bideford, Devon

J

J. W. Jardine – Leamington Spa
Nicky and Colin Jones – Dolton, Devon
Don and Gwen Jones – Dolton, Devon

L

Mrs Josephine Stewart Loam – Exeter, Devon
Jean D Lock, nee Heal – Holsworthy, Devon
Veronica Liley, nee Page – Lower Swanwick, Hampshire
Mr J. T. Lane (In Memory of), formerly the Headmaster of Hatherleigh School
Gay and Charmian Leatt – Torrington, Devon
Lynette Lewis, nee Wadland – Aspendale, Australia
Nancy Leverton – Broadclyst, Devon

M

Richard Mendham – c/o Chelfham, Bere Alston, Devon
Kerry Mullett, nee Hodge – Victoria, Australia
Julie Ann Mioch, nee Hodge – Victoria, Australia
Bridget Moger – Beaford, Devon

LIST OF SUBSCRIBERS

N
Ken and Kay North – Dolton, Devon
Louise Noble, (Lise), nee Budgett – Matlock Bath, Matlock
Derek Nancekivell – Boscastle, Cornwall
Rachel Newton, nee Davies – Sutton, Surrey
North Devon Athenaeum – Barnstaple, Devon

P
Susan Patrick, nee Luxmoore – Bourne End, Bucks
John Puddicombe – Honiton Clyst, Exeter, Devon
Mrs Ada Piper – Dolton, Devon
Alida Pollard – Yelverton, Devon
Roger Page – Sarisbury Green, Southampton

Q
Phyllis M Quick, nee Folland – Southampton, Hants

R
Steve Reader – Wallingford, Oxfordshire

S
Marion Small – Brixham, Devon
Mrs Eileen Sutton – Dolton, Devon
Major H. Sawrey-Cookson – Penrith, Cumbria
Julie Soper – Exmouth, Devon
Mary Squire, nee Ball – Northam, Devon
Gary and Valerie Skull – Dolton, Devon
David and Jackie Sweet – Foxdale, Isle of Man
Martyn Steer-Folwer – Brynsworthy, Barnstaple
Owen and Glenda (nee Wadland) Sydenham – Macksville, N.S.W., Austalia

T
Mrs Ethel Turner – Dolton, Devon
Isabel Trewin, nee Heal – Safety Bay, Western Australia

V
Keith Vodden – Corfe, Somerset

W
Stephen and Julie Wadlan – Plymouth, Devon
Vivien Wynn, nee Wadland – Bridgwater, Somerset
Colin West – Rugby, Warwickshire
Nicholas West – Upton-on-Severn, Worcs
David Wills – Henstridge, Somerset
Mrs Josephine Wills – Dolton, Devon
Andrew Wadland – Kennington
Samuel Henry and Doreen Wadland – Broadwell, Warwickshire
Martin and Angela Wadland – Boddington, Northamptonshire
Simon Wadland – Claydon, Oxfordshire
Tim Wadland – Boddington, Northamptonshire
Richard A Wadland – Tur Langton, Leicester
Richard A Wadland – Desborough, Northants
Mrs Agnes Wadland – Lower Hampt, Stoke Climand, Cornwall
David Walker – Little Petherick, Cornwall
Mr Arthur J Wadland (In Memory of) – Exeter, Devon
Trevor and Yvonne Wadland – Hunters Hill, Sydney, Australia
Robert and Samantha Wadland – Penshurst, Sydney, Australia
Geoffrey and Linden Wadland, Oatley, Sydney, Australia
Pauline Wooddisse – Dolton, Devon
Andrew Wadland – Eastbourne, East Susserx. In Memory of his Father Roy, Grandfather Arthur and Uncle Peter.
Mrs Carol Wadland Croxton, Staffordshire. In Memory of my husband Roy, who would have loved to have seen this book published.
Malcolm Wadland – Staffordshire. In memory of his father Roy, Grandfather Arthur and Uncle Peter
Pricilla West – Plymouth, Devon
David West – Bury St Edmunds, Suffolk

In Memory of Mr Roy Wadland and Mr Peter Wadland

As the author of this biography, I would also like to say that I regret that my cousins Roy and Peter are not here to see this book, due, very sadly to their untimely deaths. They were two very accomplished gentlemen, who would, had they lived longer, given so much more to society.

AMW

PRINTED AND BOUND BY LAZARUS PRESS
CADDSDOWN BIDEFORD DEVON